Growth with Equity

Strategies for Meeting Human Needs

Edited by
Mary Evelyn Jegen
and
Charles K. Wilber

261.83
G919

PAULIST PRESS
New York/Ramsey/Toronto

Royalties from this book will go to the Bread for the World Educational Fund.

Copyright © 1979 by
The Missionary Society
of St. Paul the Apostle
in the State of New York

All rights reserved. No part of this book may be reproduced or transmitted in any form or by any means, electronic or mechanical, including photocopying, recording or by any information storage and retrieval system without permission in writing from the Publisher.

Library of Congress
Catalog Card Number: 78-70818

ISBN: 0-8091-2163-8

Published by Paulist Press
Editorial Office: 1865 Broadway, New York, N.Y. 10023
Business Office: 545 Island Road, Ramsey, N.J. 07446

Printed and bound in the
United States of America

The John J. Wright Library
LA ROCHE COLLEGE
9000 Babcock Boulevard
Pittsburgh, Pa. 15237

Contents

v

VI
FURTHER THEOLOGICAL PERSPECTIVE

APPENDIX

I have the audacity to believe that peoples everywhere can have three meals a day for their bodies, education and culture for their minds, and dignity, equality and freedom for their spirits. I believe that what self-centered men have torn down other-centered men can build up. I still believe that one day mankind will bow before the altars of God and be crowned triumphant. . . . I still believe that we shall overcome.

Martin Luther King, Jr.
Nobel Peace Prize Acceptance Speech

Preface

In 1974, the United States made a proposal to the World Food Conference held at a period of international concern over a global food crisis. Our Secretary of State declared as a goal ". . . that within a decade no child will go to bed hungry, that no family will fear for its next day's bread, and that no human being's future and capacities will be stunted by malnutrition." A sustained effort, both public and private, is indispensable to prevent that declaration from becoming idle rhetoric. *Bread for the World Educational Fund* is designed to serve that long term effort.

Established in 1976, Bread for the World Educational Fund launched that same year a *Decade of Commitment on World Hunger*. This ten year program, directed to higher education communities, seeks to make world hunger a current and compelling issue for faculty, administration, and students. In some cases, this means working with a college or university which has already taken initiatives to locate the central human issue of hunger in its curriculum.

The University of Notre Dame is one such university. From the beginning it has shared its own rich human resources with *Bread for the World Educational Fund* in an effort to create programs and materials that can serve the needs of other educators. This book represents the fruit of one such effort. Well over a year of planning went into the seminar which culminated in this book.

We can never thank adequately the authors of the essays in this volume. While they represent differences of opinion on important issues, they are all characterized by what one commentator has called "informed compassion." Such writing makes for compelling reading.

Bread for the World Educational Fund is also deeply grateful to the following members of the University of Notre Dame community who gave many hours of service to the planning process for

1

the seminar: David Burrell, C.S.C., Charles Wilber, Don McNeill, C.S.C., Basil O'Leary, and Sister Jane Pitz. The seminar itself was held at Moreau Seminary on the University Campus, thanks to the gracious hospitality of the Holy Cross community there. Financial support was contributed both by the University and the Congregation of Holy Cross.

From the time the seminar *Growth with Equity* was announced, requests to participate, or at least to share in the proceedings, began to come to our office. We hope that this book will provide a useful response to those requests. We further hope that the collaborative experience represented here will urge many others involved in higher education to search for ways to relate their work to the problems of achieving growth with equity. This is a central issue in a world which still tolerates starvation and malnutrition for hundreds of millions of precious human beings.

This book should make clear the vision of *Bread for the World Educational Fund*. We recognize that hunger is a complex issue. For this reason, education on such matters as the right to food, agricultural development, international trade, and employment strategies is crucial. In the last analysis, how we act in regard to hunger depends on how well we understand it.

Our work springs from our awareness of God's love for all people. The love he has shared with us in Jesus Christ will not let us turn aside from those who suffer dehumanizing hunger. The quality of our own lives depends on the way we respond to the basic needs of the entire human family sharing our linked and limited world. We will continue to pursue our educational goals with many others who share that conviction.

Mary Evelyn Jegen
Executive Director
Bread for the World Educational Fund

Foreword

The *Bread for the World Educational Fund* teamed up with the Department of Economics at the University of Notre Dame to bring some fifty college students, faculty and thoughtful spokesmen for development together for an intensive weekend in February 1978. The Congregation of Holy Cross (Indiana Province) helped to make the seminar a reality through an assistance grant of its Apostolic Fund, and the facilities of Moreau Seminary provided the touch of informal hospitality that made the exchange so memorable.

Paul Streeten (from Oxford and the World Bank) had been lecturing at Notre Dame the previous week in the series: New Directions in Economic Development. Branko Horvat of the University of Belgrade was also present at the University as Visiting Professor for part of the spring semester. Other participants included Notre Dame faculty and students, some of whom had prepared for the conference in specific courses designed to raise the background issues, while others brought considerable expertise with them. Persons invited from beyond the University represented individuals who have long wrestled with the tangle of issues included in development, and all the participants were chosen with a view toward bringing various perspectives to bear on the questions.

The goal of the conference was to explore the many facets of development to discover the components of a sane response from all three "worlds." Hence the guiding title: Growth with Equity. The perspective chosen was that of "basic human needs," but Paul Streeten's continued clarifications, as well as Denis Goulet's and James Weaver's commentaries, kept the group from taking this perspective to represent a single approach. Three facets were scrutinized in some detail: agricultural development (Schertz, Waterston), employment strategies (Schervish, Wilber and Jame-

3

son), and international institutions (Barnet, Land, Streeten). Participants had agreed to read their drafts in advance of the seminar so that the authors would profit from an informed exchange of views. The chapters in this volume reflect that exchange, and incorporate what they can of the learning experience the weekend proved to be. The original hope of the planners: to prepare materials for classroom and discussion use by submitting individual drafts to intensive group discussion, worked out better than they dared to dream—thanks to the generosity of the resource persons, the overall preparedness of the group, and the hospitality of the surroundings. While that experience itself cannot be transmitted in a series of essays, something of the challenge of the exchange can be felt in the way these chapters deal with the different sides of those issues as they demand our respect.

Fred McEldowney, from the Office of Food Policy and Programs of the Department of State, opened the meeting with an overview of the institutions arising from the 1974 World Food Conference (printed as an appendix in this volume). Discussion of the stated perspective of the seminar—Basic Human Needs—began in earnest with Denis Goulet's searching critique of our readiness to define others' "basic needs." He scored the tensions which obtain between ways of satisfying these needs—assistance versus self-reliance—and warned us against preoccupation with material needs when the most basic human need may well be "having a meaningful existence." Regarding strategies, Goulet insisted that we can only meet basic needs when we empower the poor to make effective demands on the social systems in which they live—for they are the best judges of their needs.

James Weaver canvassed the settled inventory of basic needs—food, water, housing, health, education—to show that less developed countries will need external assistance to address these within a reasonable timetable of a quarter-century. Yet it would take only .35% of the GNP of developed nations to finance up to 50% of such a program. To that end, Weaver outlines a reformist strategy for development, including some sage observations on the local arrangements needed to assure that schemes materialize.

Lyle Schertz of the U.S. Department of Agriculture shows effectively how interdependence provides a lever for dealing with food issues, as well as a way of comprehending their complexity.

Albert Waterston outlines his scheme of integrated rural develop-ment, showing how critical a resource are trained personnel willing to share the lot of rural folk long enough to gain their trust and to train them. Colleges and universities, together with volunteer and church groups, can form a fruitful coalition for teaching, research and effective field work in this area.

Paul Schervish introduces the perspective of employment by reminding us how a pervasive policy of catering to first world needs has skewed third world production practices. A contrast of the relative periods of development germane to these two "worlds" makes that thesis all too clear. Ken Jameson and Charles Wilber explore various employment strategies, first noting how misleading a term "employment" can be. This initial discussion makes them resist identifying employment with jobs in the most visible sectors of an economy, and allows them to determine a yardstick for "more productive employment." The example of Brazil shows how an absolute increase in wage-earning jobs may only selectively benefit a country's economic well-being. Con-sequently they argue against any single strategy of integrating industry as well as the work of independent artisans into a devel-opment scenario which includes parallel technologies of vastly different sorts.

Shifting to international institutions, Richard Barnet scrutinizes the practices of agencies like the World Bank and IMF, as well as multinational corporations, for their effects on develop-ment. International agencies have a way of enforcing demands for internal reorganization with telling political implications, while some practices of multinationals can evade scrutiny. Philip Land shows how acutely trade flow and debt structures affect develop-ing countries, and offers some proposals for improving what has been a situation of virtual domination. Paul Streeten brings his experience from the World Bank to bear on clarifying some of the issues which bedevil international exchange, and offers these clarifications as another way of meeting basic human needs. (The theological reflections of John Howard Yoder at the beginning and closing sessions were unique in their power to raise questions beyond those formally addressed by the authors of the major papers.)

As mentioned earlier, the exchange occasioned by the Growth

with Equity Conference finds its way into each chapter, as individual authors reflect what they learned from the lively critique of their original drafts. But the spirit of that weekend escapes a chapter-by-chapter format. Much of it had to do with an exchange that is only possible between young and old—everyone remarked how critical was the presence of students. Yet most telling of all was the spirit which made each of us students—first of those who had reflected the most on these issues, but then of one another, as these mentors endeavored to expose the human side of every "complex" issue, displaying in their own reverence for the truth as well as the facts of these matters, how it is that all of us must work to understand basic human needs if we are to participate effectively in development. As the planners had hoped, the seminar itself became a microcosm of integrated human development, which I trust will be extended manyfold by the essays printed here. The experience itself offers an initial sounding of the ways in which colleges and universities can cooperate with voluntary groups to bring outstanding resources to bear on pressing human issues. May this effort inspire many more like it!

Whether or not the ideal of growth with equity is realized depends more than anything else upon the political will of the nations of the North. It is, in fact, a supreme test of our humanity as citizens of the Northern Hemisphere, representing three quarters of the wealth and power in this world, if we are really to address ourselves before the year 2000 to the elimination of the effects of dire poverty on the part of over a billion people living in the Fourth World. I believe that all the ideas relevant to the solution are already in place, as the following chapters will indicate, but what we really need is the political will to make it work. Without this political will, we have an ideal that forces itself upon us as the highest moral imperative of our times, and a kind of awesome new holocaust that we could prevent, but only if we will it.

Theodore M. Hesburgh, C.S.C.
President
University of Notre Dame

I
Theological Perspective

Theological Perspectives on "Growth with Equity"

John H. Yoder

It was meant seriously when the planners of the Notre Dame meeting said that the involvement of theological perspective in the consultation should not be that of a normative foundation stated a priori from which implementation should be derived, nor that of a blessing pronounced over the problem, nor an appeal to the goodwill of the participants, but rather an ongoing conversation with the other materials being studied in the consultation.

It follows very properly that these notes can be only that: notes along the way as the conference opened out from the preparatory papers and gathered around the conversational processes in small groups and plenary sessions. The sharing of these "perspectives" with the group was provided for at two occasions: one at the beginning of the second session and one at the beginning of the final discussion. The format of those impromptu introductions has been preserved in the following texts.

A "perspective" is something less easy to describe than a proclamation. My assignment is to articulate together with you something about how or from where we see things, more than about what it is that we see.

Permit me to break the subject matter down quite formally. First of all, we need to take account of matters contributing very much to our orientation but not in need of much repetition. It has been said, and needs only to be repeated, but hardly with much argument, that as Christians we have a very precise mandate which drives us into caring about hunger and about development. To say it within the biblical imagery:

We have been given a garden to share. We have been given one another with whom to share in cultivating it and in eating its fruits. We have been instructed to serve God within a history that is going somewhere, directional, not to be satisfied with stability or stagnation.

We have failed in all of those tasks.

Nonetheless, we have been restored by a series of gracious interventions, not of our own doing, so that our calling from now on is not simply to extrapolate from the initial creative impetus, but to be liberated and to liberate one another from the results of the fall.

We are called to share in the bias of God in favor of the victims, and the bias of Jesus in favor of the enemy, and the bias of the Spirit in favor of hope.

All of this has been said abundantly in the literature of the movement which our sponsoring entities both follow and lead. I could spend our time reviewing those basic common affirmations, the review would not be wasteful. Yet I believe that my primary assignment lies elsewhere.

Second, in this purely formal sifting, I should identify serious questions that reach beyond the material with which our papers deal. The closer we get to the material in the papers, the more they point beyond themselves to this further set of questions.

One way that these papers, dealing with macro-systemic analysis, point beyond themselves, is that they help us identify a set of questions with which they do not deal. There are forces which keep the best oiled and best designed macro-systems from delivering what they are supposed to deliver. Personal ego needs, hatred and power hunger, self-seeking group interests which some are willing to promote at the cost of others, susceptibility to demagoguery and aggressive rhetoric often (—usually!) make our best designs dysfunctional. There is corruption at the heart of our creativity, not only in the worst but also in the best of our human potential. To some extent it can be argued that these more personal and provincial vices are the product of larger systemic maladjustments as much as they are the causes thereof, but this does not mean that if everybody were well fed selfishness would evaporate. Now how do we deal with this radical sinfulness? For some it is specifically the task of religion to deal with personal virtues and the cultivation of styles of problem solving and industriousness that will make bad systems more livable and good systems viable. I think we want to demur from any such division of labor that would tell us to let religion produce virtuous people and then economics would tell us what structures they should build. Yet on the other hand we do admit that the economists are not going to produce the virtuous people, and that the economic system will not save itself without them.

There is one clear crisis which we cannot avoid in the realm that we are now studying. In preparation for this weekend, trying to read these papers as the ordinary concerned American would read them, this crisis seemed to me to be visible just under the surface most of the time.

The predominant vision of the course of history which has molded Western post-Christendom culture, American culture perhaps most pointedly, is what I might call the paradigm of power. Whatever needs to be done can be done and we are the ones to do it. The confidence that history moves forward and the confidence that God has blessed us in particular interlock in a spiralling way. Because we have prospered we know that the world is progressing. Because progress is the law of world history, we know that the way in which our success was obtained was right. We tend to take that rightness as meaning both technical correctness and moral rectitude.

This notion of success as the model of human experience has, of course, many sources. Some of them are as old as biblical religion and others are as recent as the energy explosion precipitated by fossil fuels. Some of its components have been specific cultural strengths like the organization capacity of the post-puritan entrepreneur, the engineer, and the military technology which permitted the growth of empire. Others have been simply the advantage of expropriated resources, especially the gold and then the natural wealth of the new world. However spirituality, economics, piracy and poetry have combined, the lesson has been solidly learned. Anything needing to be done can be done and we are the ones to do it. God is the name for the power that confirms that mandate and enables that confidence.

It follows from all this, according to ordinary logic, that any-

thing which cannot succeed or at least anything which does not
have a relatively great chance of success does not justify the
investment of effort. We are still feeding the hungry and empower-
ing the poor as a possible target. President Hesburgh encourages
us to believe in the manageability of a global project which would
have basic human needs met before the year 2000, if the cause is
tackled properly. This projection, like all of our papers, takes for
granted a system-immanent analysis of how things work and what
is possible. They thus stayed within the heritage of the Western
tradition of progress as the way to understand meaningful human
effort. That model has abundant rootage in our Western historical
experience, and especially in the way that said history has been
written up by its beneficiaries.

But peeking around the edges of several of the papers one sees
the signals of doubt about the feasibility of such a goal, or even
about whether we are fundamentally gaining any ground toward it.
That is in itself still a question within the system-immanent
analysis. The question that comes within the purview of my "perspective" assignment is whether it makes any difference whether
or not we expect to succeed. Does it make any difference in our
optimism whether it is supported by social science projections?
What if the feasibility of that program which would lead us to have
met all basic needs by 1999 were seen to have miscalculated very
seriously certain linkages or certain coefficients? What if the notion of the normalcy of progress which has formed our total Western personality were shown to have been the product of a very
narrowly selective reading of cultural history, possible only for
those who have been the beneficiaries of a fundamentally exploitative world system? What if the possibility of running that optimistic
vision through until 1999 were crucially dependent upon the operation of forces completely beyond our control or within the control
of people with other interests? If it were a losing battle to feed
everyone by 1999 would that be any less right?

One segment of the power-for-progress paradigm is the ability
to reduce problems to scientifically manageable proportions by
developing the sciences which enable us to analyze and then the
skills which let us manipulate. Applied science, proceeding by the
reduction of complex events to mechanical and mathematical

models, enables us to modify the genes of our crops and flocks, to multiply the potency of our vitamins and our fertilizers, and to fly to the moon. The next frontier is to bring to bear upon the problem of poverty that same scientific power, by engineering in places where it has not yet happened a replication of the process of development which has made some of us rich already. That replication will be difficult because the circumstances are less ideal elsewhere but it should not be impossible in principle.

It is with this confidence in mind that we look to our economists. Most of the papers in this collection were prepared by people for whom the discipline of economics is a professional identity in banking or the university: The others as well even though their disciplines be those of sociology, agronomy, or the philosophy of culture still have written for our purposes in the same key, leading us through the same analyses of how processes work and how we might get from here to there.

This power model of implicit analysis is further heightened in these papers because the subject matter is centered on the most global structures of society, especially the economic. Any discussion about how the structures work and how we evaluate the way they work tends to foster the implicit assumption that we are free or maybe even responsible to reform the structures at will. To say that a structure is oppressive is practically tantamount to saying we must do away with it. This is still more the case when there is an actual discussion going on about how legislators or world bureaucrats do develop new structures or change old ones, how patterns of market manipulation have developed for reasons which can be recounted, and when the conference participants have the privilege of listening to some of the senior staff who had a voice in those processes of improving structures.

The crisis of which we need to speak arises at the point where that success paradigm begins to be questioned. I can only allude in slogan form to some of the ways, most of them quite obvious, in which that questioning has surfaced.

What if the experts in a given scientific discipline differ among themselves? The progress and power paradign assumes that the technocrats can get together on what needs to be done. That is why we can afford to leave it to them to do it, since there is no deep debate about what to do. That is why their technocratic programming is seen to be a part of the nature of things, a kind of natural theology of what to do in the economic world, with no serious doubt as to whether those are the rules. If, however, economics should turn out to be a branch not so much of statistics as of ethical philosophy, then our question is not how to mobilize people to do what everyone knows needs to be done, but rather which prophet to listen to and which demons to exorcise.

Ever since Constantine in principle, and ever since Aquinas in spelled-out theory, the relationship of nature and grace or of technique and morality has been such that we trust the people who know about nature to tell us where to start. We trust the economists to tell us about economic development and the nutritionists to tell us what people should have to eat. Then the religionists try to stir us up to do those good things.

That smooth division of labor fits well within the progress imagery of a Christendom getting more and more on top of its problems. It fits less in a world out of control, or even in a world out of sync.

Our dismay is at least triple when our cultural self-confidence thus reaches its borders.

1. The experience itself becomes infinite in its complexity, cancerous in its increasing ramifications and the new confusions it creates. The tools of analysis need themselves to be analyzed in an infinite regression of methodological introspection.

2. Engineering expertise points beyond itself to politics. This was the most evident impression for me as an amateur: we face the lesson that for socio-economic development to be authentic "people have to learn to do it on their own." Yet for a disadvantaged economy to let that happen would demand very complex market controls, which even the developed economies do not have and which (my gloss) would lend themselves very easily to being corrupted.

3. Politics points beyond itself to the mystery of depravity: pride, the abuse of power, alienation within the person and between persons.

How then do we explain that so wholesome and affirmative a mandate as "the fire is for you to take" should have so run amok that we have growth without equity and without order? Perhaps some of the reason is inadequate technical know-how but there is also a flaw in the will. Prometheus was (partly) a destroyer after all.

But when the great Western dream breaks down we cannot simply (unfortunately) go back to Go. We are worse off than before. Jesus once said parabolically that if the space opened by exorcism is not filled wholesomely, the place of the first expelled demon will be filled by seven others and "the last state of that man is worse than the first." Hendrik Berkhof has seen this as pre-figuring a phenomenon in modern cultural history: the way crea-turely values once subdued to servanthood again become au-tonomous, so that their dominion over us is greater than before they were sobered by the proclamation of Christ (if the mythic tone of this language seems strange I can only refer the reader to Berkhof's *Christ and the Powers*).

If we counted on solving all our problems with the resources of Western cultural power, our backlash will naturally be angry, frustration with ourselves and with those whom we blame for our failure, with a resulting readiness to cut corners and to violate the dignity of persons, institutions, and some of the very values we claim to defend.

This observation now enables me to refocus my assignment. What we need a "perspective" on is not whether we should share, or even why we should share. It is rather how to deal with our dismay in the fact of the inadequacy of our resource for moving toward sharing. At this point it is not enough to say "religion" provides "motivation" only in the sense of the overarching formal imperatives to do good, or some inexplicable drive to care which some persons get through religious experience. Nor is it enough to assure ourselves of a sense of forgiveness or peace in the midst of our ongoing inadequacies, nor even of a power to keep on hoping and willing the good.

On the other hand it would be too much to try to draw from specifically religious sources some prescriptive models for the way to share (although some might hold that they are there: the Genesis story is about economic development and Leviticus talks about the institutional redistribution of the Jubilee).

Between the too little and the too much, between mere

motivation and necessarily anachronistic prescriptions, what is it that we can still receive from a believing identity? The hypothesis I offer is that we might expect our Christian faith to suggest resources for paradigm change: a readiness to be more imaginative in reshaping our sense of search.

It is common enough recently to interpret the process of the major intellectual disciplines as consisting not simply in the accumulation of more of the same kind of data but as a series of changes in fundamental interpretative paradigms: this is most demonstrable in some of the natural sciences but it is just as true (although less neat) in letters and the soft sciences. In the face of problems insoluble in the terms in which they had been formulated, the way forward comes not by forcing the data, or raising the ante, or trying harder, nor hurrying, nor praying but by recasting the question so as to gain a new perspective on what might count as an answer. Might it be that this resource of open flexibility for paradigm change would be what our faith would bring to the obligation to share the fruits of the garden with one another?

II
Basic Human Needs
Perspective

Measuring and Meeting Basic Needs

James H. Weaver

This paper is divided into three sections. The first section deals with basic needs as the new goal of development. In this section, estimates of the global dimensions of the problem are presented. We then raise the question of whether we can measure basic needs on a global basis and whether we can estimate the costs of meeting these needs.

The second section of the paper examines three broad strategies for meeting basic needs. The first strategy is the traditional capital-oriented strategy aimed at maximizing the growth of GNP. The second strategy is a revolutionary socialist alternative. The third strategy is a reformist strategy which calls for growth *with* equity.

The final section will summarize the arguments that have been made and will present the conclusions.

I
THE NEW GOAL OF DEVELOPMENT

There appears to be a consensus emerging in the development community. The consensus is that the goal of development should be to meet the basic needs of every person born on the planet. These needs are: food specified in terms of calories—specific by age, by sex, by occupation, by geographic region; potable water in reasonable proximity to people's houses; clothing and shelter which are adequate to the locality in which people live; medical care which includes preventive medicine, sanitation, health services, nutrition, population services; and education which prepares people for more productive lives. Meeting basic needs can be

19

seen as an organizing principle around which systematically to organize our thinking and our development efforts.

This new consensus is reflected in the agreements reached at recent world conferences, i.e., the World Food Conference in Rome, Habitat in Vancouver, Water in Mar del Plat, Argentina in 1977, and the International Labor Organization Conference in Geneva in 1976. The emerging consensus is also reflected in the Foreign Assistance Act of 1973 and World Bank policy papers. The academic literature on development also reflects this growing consensus.

This new goal of development contrasts sharply with the old goal which was to increase per capita income. It was assumed that if incomes went up, basic needs would be met.

The Dimensions of the Problem

The World Bank staff argues that even though the less developed countries have had an impressive rate of growth of per capita income in the last 25 years, over one-half of the world's population still cannot meet their minimum basic needs and the staff has recently completed global estimates of basic needs by sectors, i.e., food, shelter, medical care, education, etc. What do these estimates show?

Food

When we look at food needs, it is estimated that there are approximately 930 million people who are presently getting less than the minimum daily requirement of 2,350 calories.

The Bank staff estimates that the total investment cost of meeting the food requirements would be $28.4 billion (1975 dollars used in all estimates) for the period from 1980 to the year 2000. This would be an annual cost of $1.4 billion. In addition to these investment costs there would be recurrent costs which would be about $5.7 billion per year. This would mean a total recurrent cost of $113.6 billion for the period 1980 to 2000. However, the staff argues that present world production is already adequate to feed everyone if it were distributed more equally.

Water

The basic need for drinking water is defined as reasonable access to water that does not contain substances harmful to the health or make the water unacceptable to people. The Bank estimates that there are approximately 1.2 billion people who do not have access to such drinking water at the present time. The staff presents estimates that reasonably safe supplies of drinking water are unavailable for at least one-fifth of the world's population based on data presented to the recent U.N. Water Conference held in Argentina in March of 1977.

Several alternative estimates of the cost of providing safe water are presented. Total investment requirements for 1980–2000 would range from $50 billion to $135 billion depending on the alternative chosen. Recurrent costs of $45 billion would be necessary.

It is pointed out that in the past the developing countries have traditionally provided much of the investment themselves in this sector. However, the percentage of the population served has remained very low, particularly in rural areas. The staff estimates that if everyone were to be provided with safe water by 2000, up to $76 billion would have to be provided by external sources of finance.

Housing

The basic need for shelter is defined as the need for permanent shelter which protects human beings from harmful climatic influences and other dangerous factors in their natural environment. This would vary enormously from culture to culture, but basic housing needs represent the minimum socially acceptable dwelling standards among the poorest strata of any society. The Bank staff finds no reliable estimates of people deprived of basic housing but they estimate that it is probably at least 800 million people.

The Bank staff uses estimates made at the Habitat Conference that by 1980 there will be approximately 955 million people living in sub-standard housing. This would translate into the need for approximately 106 million housing units by 1980, and 218 million between 1980 and 2000. The cost of meeting the housing needs over the period 1980 to 2000 would be $218 billion based on an average cost of meeting housing needs of $1,000 per unit. The staff has made low and high estimates of the recurrent costs of housing. The low estimate would be $178 billion for the period 1980 to 2000. The high estimate would be $394 billion.

Health

Basic health care is defined as public and private measures needed to prevent and cure the most common avoidable or curable diseases and other forms of bodily harm. The Bank staff estimates that there are approximately 800 million people presently deprived of these basic health services.

The total investment cost of meeting the health needs of the poor would range from $25 to $29 billion during the period 1980 to 2000. Annual average recurrent costs would vary from $11 billion on the low side to $19 billion on the high side. These estimates are based on the Bank's experience in health projects in 13 developing countries. The strategy laid out is based on extending the coverage of the primary health care system, increasing the responsiveness of existing health posts and district hospitals to the needs of the primary health workers, and planning the extension of primary care by supplementing the role played by traditional village healers. Heavy emphasis is placed on controlling tropical diseases.

Education

Basic education is defined as the education which provides functional, flexible, and low cost education for those whom the formal system cannot reach or has already passed by. The target group includes, in addition to school aged children, women, adults who missed schooling, etc. It is estimated that there are approximately 1.1 billion people in this category, including 300 million children presently out of school and about 800 million adult illiterates.

During the past few decades the staff argues that the proportion of adult illiterates and out of school children in the LDCs has fallen. Their numbers have increased in absolute terms, however. Overall illiteracy in LDCs fell from about 60% in 1960 to 50% in 1975. However, there is a wide disparity in literacy rates within the Third World. In some countries, as much as 95% of the population is literate and in others as little as 11% of the adult population is literate.

The basic education strategy of the Bank accords higher priority to universal coverage than to depth of education. Its aim is to provide the basic literacy and numeracy skills essential for a productive life. A four year cycle is considered adequate to develop essential basic skills on a permanent basis and is chosen over the traditional six year cycle for reasons of economy.

The program also has a component of training for adults in production skills. This training would take place in the field and on the job. It is argued that much of the instruction could be provided by mass media. The staff estimates the investment cost for education at $51 billion and the recurrent cost at $196 billion over the period 1980 to 2000.

Global Estimates

The staff argues, first of all, that providing for the financial costs of basic needs, though not a small matter, is probably relatively easy in comparison with the political, organizational, manpower and other problems which have to be solved. Given that introduction, the total investment requirements for the production of the five basic goods and services amount to approximately $380 billion for the period 1980 to 2000. This would be approximately 6% of the world's income in 1975. The annual investment cost amounts to only .3% of world income. The estimated annual investment cost would amount to only 5% of global defense spending ($375 billion in 1975). If the nation states could somehow free themselves from the present insecurity they all feel, or even reduce this insecurity, there would be ample resources available for meeting basic needs.

The basic needs investments required for low income countries equals 55% of their gross domestic investment or 52% of government revenues. Thus, low income countries could not be expected to finance such investments on their own.

The recurrent expenditures are much larger than the capital costs. The staff argues that making provisions for recurrent cost may be more important for the success of the basic needs programs than making the initial capital outlay. For all developing countries, recurrent costs are estimated to range between $28 to $40 billion per year. The estimates of total recurrent costs for the period 1980 to 2000 range from a low of $565 billion to a high of $789 billion.

When the investment and recurrent costs are added together the average cost per year ranges from $47 to $59 billion and the total for the 20 years ranges from $943 billion to $1.2 trillion. The total cost of meeting basic needs would take approximately 12% to 16% of the average GNP of the LDCs, 80% to 105% of their gross domestic investment, and 85% to 110% of their government revenues.

External Assistance

These figures indicate that a global basic needs program, if it is to be implemented in a few decades, cannot be financed by the poor countries themselves. Such a program must rely heavily on transfers from the rich countries.

At present development assistance is on the order of $13 to $14 billion a year. Much of this is not for basic needs related projects. Development assistance would not only have to be increased, it would have to undergo a radical transformation if basic needs were to be met by the year 2000.

If the rich nations underwrite about 50% of the additional cost of the basic needs programs this would require about $22 to $30 billion a year or about .35% of their future GNPs. Some people in the Bank argue that these amounts can be provided if there is a real increase in official development assistance (ODA) and if at least the incremental ODA is directed mainly toward the poorest nations and toward basic needs programs.

However, the staff reminds us again that the requirement for foreign assistance should not be overemphasized. The more important issue is the crucial *internal* changes that are needed within the LDCs before basic needs programs can be implemented with any success. Much of the investment and maintenance efforts of basic needs projects must be generated domestically through taxation, public works, or self-help. The staff argues that the satisfaction of basic needs is fundamentally not a matter of financial resources but of mobilizing human beings by employing the right policies, technologies and institutions.

Can We Estimate Global Needs?

It is necessary to read the estimates of basic needs carefully and to analyze the assumptions on which these estimates are made. The staff papers are quite circumspect in their claims to present the reality of global needs. Many limitations and warnings are listed. In some sectors, it is admitted that no basis exists for making global estimates.

It is also clear that there are many alternative ways to go about meeting basic needs. The method chosen will determine the costs incurred. So, the estimates of costs are even more speculative than are estimates of needs.

Given all these data limitations, why should global estimates of basic needs be made? There is a compelling reason. Until such estimates are made and discussed seriously by policy makers, the requisite data will not be generated. The Bank has made an heroic effort to present estimates and it is to be hoped that these estimates will provoke agencies and governments to generate more realistic data.

Country Estimates

The Bank has prepared country estimates of basic needs and a strategy for meeting these needs for Pakistan. This is a very promising and provocative document and indicates the best way to estimate basic needs, that is, country by country. Hopefully, the Bank's efforts will lead to publication of country by country estimates of basic needs by sector.

II
ALTERNATIVE STRATEGIES FOR MEETING BASIC NEEDS

Traditional Strategy

The first strategy is a continuation of the traditional approach which has been followed during the last 25 years, that is, the capital oriented strategy which emphasizes capital as the missing ingredient and investment in industry as the key to development. Benefits will trickle down to the poor.

The advocates of this strategy argue that efforts were successful. They cite the recent study by David Morawetz (*Twenty-Five Years of Economic Development*) as evidence for their claim that development has been successful.

They argue that the main problem in the past was that most poor countries did not allow markets to work properly and that the solution is to get the prices right. If wages are restrained and costs of capital are increased, profit maximizing capitalists will choose to employ labor rather than capital. If foreign exchange rates are brought into equilibrium, the importation of capital will be discouraged and exports will be encouraged. If agricultural prices are allowed to rise to world market prices, farmers will have an incentive to produce and will produce food necessary to feed the people. People will use their increased income to meet their basic needs themselves.

It is argued that this is the only strategy that has worked over time and there is much to commend it. Taiwan is cited as an example of a country that got prices right and had labor intensive industrialization. Taiwan is a classic case of the success of trickle down development meeting basic needs.

Critics of the traditional approach have argued that this approach has led to rising unemployment, growing concentration of income and even to an absolute worsening of the incomes of the poor. Even some of the defenders of the traditional approach would agree that the traditional approach is not reaching the landless in less developed countries and it is currently estimated that there are approximately 350 million people in the world without access to land.

The Revolutionary Alternative

Many people would argue that the only way to meet basic needs is through a complete social, political, and economic revolution. The strongest point of this argument is that it is impossible to bring about equitable growth without equitable distribution of assets first. Land reform is a precondition for growth that will benefit the rural poor and the landless in less developed countries. A fair amount of evidence exists to support this point of view. Both Adleman and Morawetz argue that historically equitable growth has only occurred where there has been equitable ownership of assets first.

The debate, then, is over whether land reform and asset redistribution can take place without revolution. The revolutionaries argue that it cannot. They cite China as one of the few countries where basic needs have been met and this came about *after* a revolution.

The reformers argue that there are many cases where basic needs have been met without revolutions. They cite Japan, Israel, Taiwan, Korea, Hong Kong, Sri Lanka, Singapore, Costa Rica and Kerala as examples. Second, they argue that revolutions simply are not in the cards for many less developed countries. Thus, something has to be done by way of reform if millions of people are not to be denied access to basic needs for decades. Third, they argue that revolutions have not been unqualified successes in meeting basic needs and in guaranteeing and insuring human rights. They cite the record of 20th century revolutions including Russia, Mexico, Cambodia, Bolivia, Algeria, Cuba, China, Viet Nam, Laos, Angola, Mozambique, Ethiopia. They argue that this is certainly a mixed record in terms of success. Revolutions are always painful but are not always successful in meeting basic needs.

The defenders of the revolutionary alternative would argue that the cases cited for equitable growth without revolution are all special cases. They would argue that land reform is impossible in poor countries without destroying the power of the feudal elites who now control those societies.

The third alternative is the reformist one and will be referred to as the growth with equity alternative. The reformists may disagree on the correct alternative to follow but they agree on one thing; meeting basic needs *can* be done in a reformist strategy.

Growth with Equity: Reform

The reformist strategy for meeting basic needs is just now emerging. There is no agreed on approach for meeting basic needs within the reformist strategy; however, a degree of consensus is emerging concerning the elements of such a strategy. There are four different levels.

First, there is an approach for the rural sector. Second, urban development is necessary. There are three broad themes or goals of national policy: increasing productivity, employment and incomes; meeting basic needs directly; and mobilizing the people for self-reliant development. At the international level, a new international economic order is necessary if basic needs are to be met.

Rural Development

Within the rural sector there are essentially two approaches to meeting basic needs, agriculture first and integrated rural development. The agriculture first strategy has been outlined by John Mellor in *The New Economics of Growth*, and by Bruce Johnston and Peter Kilby in *Agriculture and Structural Transformation*. This strategy argues that if basic needs are to be met, agriculture rather than industry should be the leading sector. Most of the poor people are in rural areas and most of the people in poor countries are involved in agriculture. So agriculture must be the leading sector. Much of the basis for the Mellor strategy comes from the experience of the Indian Punjab.

This strategy requires, first of all, fairly equitable ownership of land. It doesn't require equal access to land but fairly wide distribution of land ownership. In many countries a precondition is land reform.

The second aspect of this approach is emphasis upon technological innovation in agriculture. These technological innovations should be biological in character, i.e., breakthroughs in seeds, fertilizer, cultivation, and irrigation practices. These technological innovations will be adopted by middle income farmers, i.e., people who own some land and who will respond to technological opportunities.

In addition to the need for technological innovation, the agriculture first approach requires the extension of credit, development of markets and extension programs that will reach poor farmers.

Once farmers adopt technological innovations, agricultural production will increase.

These innovations are not very labor intensive in and of themselves. But the middle income farmers will spend their increased incomes on labor intensive goods; agricultural goods such as dairy products, fruit, and vegetables, and labor intensive industrial goods such as transistor radios, bicycles, and textiles. Thus the demand for these labor intensive goods will generate employment and through employment, income.

There will be a closed self-reinforcing system with no need for government intervention to regulate farm prices. This can be diagrammed as follows:

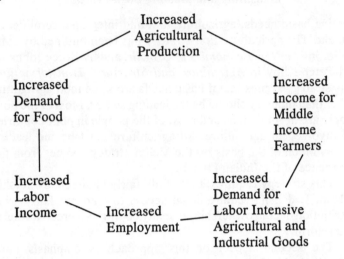

In addition to agricultural development there must be rural infrastructure to allow the system to operate: irrigation projects, farm to market roads, and so on. Such projects will generate employment and income for workers as well.

There must also be a significant degree of industrialization, e.g., cement and fertilizer production. So there are three components—agricultural production, rural infrastructure and rural industrialization. In addition, Mellor urges the less developed countries to export labor-intensive goods to pay for the capital-intensive goods they will need.

One of the problems with this approach is that it is so complex. It requires a high degree of coordination and control on the part of government. Some critics have also charged that it is a trickle down approach, the first beneficiaries are the middle income farmers and then the benefits trickle down to workers. People ask, "Why will trickle down work any better in agriculture than it did in industry?" (See Griffin.)

A variation of the Agriculture First approach is the integrated rural development approach of Albert Waterston. He argues that if there is agricultural development only, as in the Green Revolution, the rich will reap the benefits for they can take advantage of the new technology because they can afford the new seeds and the fertilizer. This would simply widen the gap between the rich and the poor. On the other hand, a basic needs approach which provides people with health care, education, food, etc., inculcates a welfare mentality and increased dependency. Waterston cites Sri Lanka and Tanzania as countries where services were provided to people thus slowing down growth since there is little incentive to produce. So he argues that these two components must be brought together in a program of integrated rural development with agricultural components, social infrastructure, and social services.

Waterson has analyzed hundreds of cases of rural development and he finds that there are six elements in successful rural development which benefit the poor.

The first element is an agricultural technology that is not only yield-increasing but also labor-intensive. This will not be as attractive to the large farmers but will be useful in increasing the incomes of the small farmers.

Second, there must be minor development projects that use surplus labor in building schools, roads, dams, irrigation projects, clinics, etc. This generates employment and increases productivity in the rural sector.

The third component is rural small-scale industry. These industries are also labor-intensive and they can produce three types of goods. They can process agriculture products, e.g., canning factories and so on. They can provide the inputs needed for agriculture, such as mixing feed or fertilizer. Third, they can produce small consumer goods which can be marketed in the rural areas.

The fourth element which Waterston finds in all successful projects is self-reliance. People have to do it on their own. In fact he argues that there is a negative relationship between outside help and success. The more outside help the project gets the less likelihood there is of success.

The fifth element is a new form of governmental organization. If the line ministries—health, agriculture, education, roads, communication, etc.—run projects down in the villages, there simply won't be successful rural development. There must be a local organization that has control over these aspects and is responsive to local people and their needs.

The sixth element is regional planning which undertakes to

develop market towns, development centers and so on, which will process agriculture goods and will provide inputs for the villages. The gap between the village and the city must be bridged.

A variant of integrated rural development is the bottlenecks first approach. In this approach the government is prepared to deal with any of the needs of the rural sector, but first assesses the situation and concentrates on those aspects which are the crucial bottlenecks in increasing agricultural production. Once this bottleneck is removed then other bottlenecks can be eliminated, etc.

Waterston's approach is quite complex organizationally. It is very difficult to conceive of bringing about the kind of organization at the local level that can carry out all of these functions, e.g., the Tanzanian experiment in decentralization. It requires a high degree of coordination on the part of government. It is also apparent that the possibility of asset redistribution is a key to the success of this approach. Thus this is an issue that must be faced. Integrated rural development schemes have had high costs per benefited family. Thus, they cannot be replicated.

Urban Development

The second level is the urban sector. This sector in turn has four subsectors. First, there is the housing component. A crucial precondition for success in meeting the housing needs of the poor is that they have tenure. Once people have title to their housing, they will begin to improve it, they will buy fixtures and furniture and this will lead to a multiplier effect throughout the informal sector that serves slum dwellers.

There are two alternatives for meeting the housing needs of the urban poor. One is a sites and services approach. The government provides the site and the services of water, electricity, sewage, streets, etc. The slum dweller is then provided a loan to build his own house.

The alternative approach is slum upgrading. In this approach, slum dwellers are given title to their house and are provided with credit and other inducements to upgrade their dwellings. Services such as electricity, water, etc., may be provided in this approach.

The second component of the urban development approach is small scale enterprises. The main input government provides to small scale enterprises is credit. In addition, there may be some extension or assistance in accounting and bookkeeping. Preference is given to those enterprises that employ the most people, or have a higher than average labor to output ratio.

The third component of the urban development approach is emphasis on infrastructure. This involves providing electricity, water, streets, telecommunications, etc., to the urban areas. It is very difficult to assess the direct beneficiaries of such projects. But some effort has been made in this direction. It turns out that telephones are one of the crucial aspects of slum upgrading and housing projects. People need access to telephones in order to find and keep jobs.

The final component of the urban development approach is industry. As in the small scale enterprises component, preference is given to industries that have a high labor component. Capital intensive industries are discouraged, and labor intensive industries are encouraged.

National Level

1. *Increasing Production and Incomes.* At the national level, there are three main goals or objectives. The first is to increase production, employment, and incomes. Basic needs strategies cannot be financed unless there is increased production and incomes.

Different theories have been developed as to how to most effectively increase production and incomes. First, there are those who emphasize employment generation. The second emphasis is on redistribution from growth of productivity. The third emphasis is on human resource development. Each of these will be analyzed in turn.

The employment generation approach grew out of the International Labor Organization (ILO) missions which were sent to various countries—Colombia, Kenya, Sri Lanka, etc. These missions discovered widespread and growing unemployment despite

THE JOHN J. WRIGHT LIBRARY

increases of GNP. They also discovered the informal sector, i.e., petty traders, tailors, retailers, carpenters, and so on, groups which had substantial entrepreneurial ability but whose main problem was a lack of capital. The ILO argued that one key to growth with equity was to switch emphasis from growth of GNP to emphasis on employment generation, and to do this partly through encouraging the informal sector and using intermediate or appropriate technology. Recent studies by Liedholm, *et al.*, in Africa confirm the ILO findings that small scale labor intensive industries are indeed efficient and profitable and suffer mainly from discriminatory interest charges for borrowed capital. This is, perhaps, the first empirical evidence that small is beautiful.

From a slightly different vantage, an enormous literature has emerged on the use of appropriate technology. The gist of the argument is that past development efforts were hampered by the use of capital intensive technology imported from developed countries—often as a result of foreign aid, or some other form of dependency relationship. The technology was associated with the West, with modernity, with efficiency, and thus was preferred to more profitable local technologies of a more labor-intensive nature. Studies by Wells and Thomas provide evidence for this claim.

Capital intensive technology created little employment and that was only for local elites. Income from production went to capital owners and it thereby exacerbated the income distribution problem in these countries.

There are two approaches to dealing with this problem. The first which is represented most clearly by Schumacher and the Intermediate Technology group is that there must be concerted effort to develop intermediate or appropriate technologies which can be incorporated in the development efforts of all countries, certainly including the underdeveloped countries.

Schumacher's case is a very strong one in favor of a technology which improves labor productivity, uses local resources, minimizes the use of non-renewable resources, and produces goods intended for local markets. It is in essence small-scale, self-help development. This appeal has met with political support in the developed countries in part because intermediate technology is no threat to multinational corporations and is not designed to produce exports to compete with U.S. manufactured goods.

A second approach sees the problem of choice of technology in terms of the price signals to producers. They find a series of distortions which favor capital: over-valued exchange rates, government subsidies to capital, local minimum wage legislation or social service programs which raise the price of labor artificially, and an interest rate policy which maintains artificially low interest rates. Thus they suggest that the manner of obtaining appropriate and labor-using technology is to remove these market distortions: maintain low wages, raise interest rates, and liberalize foreign exchange and tax policies. If these steps are taken, appropriate, labor-intensive technology will be chosen by profit-maximizing capitalists as happened after such reforms in Taiwan in the late 1950s (Ranis). Changes in factor prices will also lead to a different choice of products tilting demand to more labor-intensive products (Pack, 1974). As should be apparent, it is not always easy to distinguish this "prices right" group from the exponents of the traditional strategy.

2. *Redirecting Investment.* A second approach has been formulated by Chenery and separately by the ILO (in the Kenya report). In Chenery's formulation, emphasis is placed on the central role of capital formation. He argues that the poor must have greater capital in order to have the income which can meet their needs. Thus the policy thrust is toward a reorientation of capital formation away from large-scale centralized projects to types of investments which will relate directly to the poor; education, credit access, public facilities, etc. Command over this type of wealth will increase the productivity of the poor and thereby increase their income. In the short run this may come at the expense of growth; however, in the long run, the increased productivity and income of the poor will raise the incomes of all members of the society. Since even the well-off members of society will receive long term benefits from this "trickle up" strategy, they are not so likely to oppose it as they would a direct effort at asset redistribution.

If investment can be directed toward projects that are labor-intensive and which also meet basic human needs, over a period of time there will be a significant improvement in the lot of the poor majority. This approach is spelled out in Chenery, et al., in Chapter 2. They also suggest there that the indicator of development be a weighted growth rate of income, where the income of the poor is given a greater weight.

3. *Human Resource Development.* The third national approach is the human resource development approach proposed by Irma Adelman. This requires land reform as a precondition for development. Adelman argues that a necessary starting point is redistribution of productive assets—land and physical capital—as occurred in Japan, Taiwan and Korea. Provision must also be made to ensure continued access for the poor once the redistribution has taken place.

The next element of this strategy is a massive program to develop human resources as in South Korea. In 1964, the educational level of the Korean population was three times that of an average underdeveloped country at Korea's level of per capita GNP. This emphasis on human capital creation will inevitably be accompanied by a decade or so of slow growth of GNP, resulting in social tension, unrest and political instability. Thus, the strategy calls for a strong government which can effectively deal with these problems.

Following the creation of human capital, countries must undertake a human resource intensive industrialization and growth program. Small countries will produce for the international market, while larger countries will produce labor and skill-intensive goods for their own domestic market. The high rate of employment generated by industrialization will provide the income which will lead to a demand for the goods produced and will ensure a wide distribution of benefits.

The final stages of this process require a rapid rate of growth. That is, once past the industrialization stage, countries must grow at five or six percent a year in order to attain equity.

There are problems with this approach. It is easy to call for a strong government that is devoted to redistribution of assets and to the interests of the poor. It is another thing to get that kind of a government. And a question that is increasingly important today is the likelihood of finding such a government that will also enhance, expand, and guarantee the human rights of its people.

It should be pointed out that the human resource strategy brings the role of women to the forefront of thinking on development. For it is ludicrous to think of such a strategy unless it incorporates this group which is most often disenfranchised despite its majority status.

Meeting Basic Needs Directly

A second goal of national policy is to meet the basic needs of the poor directly. Everyone agrees that production and incomes must be increased. But, it has been found from experience that this isn't enough.

Why doesn't increasing employment meet basic needs? Many people in LDCs are not only unemployed, they are unemployable—the old, the sick, the disabled, children not part of households. These people will not be benefited by an employment approach, yet they have basic needs, too. The employment generation strategy is also deficient in that the problem is not really one of unemployment in poor countries. Only people who are fairly well-off can be unemployed in poor countries. The poor work all the time just to keep body and soul together. So the problem is not unemployment, it is unremunerative employment.

Why doesn't increasing income meet basic needs? Many basic needs can only be supplied by the public sector—sanitation, potable water, sewage, preventive medicine, education, etc. Increased income will not allow people to secure these services. In addition, people moving from subsistence to a money economy are not very capable consumers, especially in areas of nutrition and health. There are many examples of increased employment and incomes being accompanied by declining nutritional levels, e.g., reduction in breast feeding of infants.

A strategy aimed at meeting basic needs directly can, thus, meet basic needs at much lower levels of per capita income than can reliance on raising incomes. Although the evidence is not clear, it appears that China, Sri Lanka, and Kerala have met basic needs at quite low levels of per capita incomes.

Outlines of a Basic Needs Strategy

The first specific country proposal for meeting basic needs has now been prepared for Pakistan by World Bank staff members. Thus, we are able to see the elements of a basic needs strategy in concrete terms.

This strategy calls for meeting basic needs for food, shelter and clothing by increasing the incomes of the poor. It is found that 85% of additional income going to the poor is spent on meeting these three needs. However, the health, education, and sanitation needs must be provided by the public sector.

The strategy for increasing incomes for the poor involves three elements. First, great emphasis is placed on increasing the productivity of small farmers. Second, large scale industrial development is deemphasized in favor of small scale enterprises. Third, physical infrastructure such as highways and railways are deemphasized in favor of rural roads and rural electrification. The strategy paper calls for abandoning various industrial and infrastructure complexes by name.

The strategy paper calls for large increases in expenditure for education, health and sanitation. These programs are desirable in their own right but are also proposed in an effort to reduce population growth rates.

The implementation of the basic needs strategy calls for strengthening local government. People must participate in decision making at all levels.

The proponents of this basic needs strategy argue that it will not slow growth. In fact, they argue that by mobilizing underutilized resources, this strategy will lead to more rapid growth than the strategy now being followed.

Issues in Meeting Basic Needs

Won't services designed for the poor be hijacked by the rich? No doubt some of them will. There are examples of this everywhere in credit schemes for small farmers, education programs, etc. However, there are also some programs designed to benefit the poor which actually do reach the poor. This is one of the crucial problems in the basic needs approach—how to design delivery systems that do reach the poor, and how to structure services so that the linkages of various services can be taken advantage of to achieve a synergistic effect.

Another very difficult question is the combination of centralization and decentralization which is best for meeting basic needs. If the program is not based on self-help and self-reliance it becomes a welfare scheme and produces a welfare mentality and increased dependency. And yet if we wait for the poor to organize themselves to meet their basic needs we know there is going to be a very long wait. So there has to be a mix of outside intervention and local participation. We need to learn much more about how to bring this off.

How do we get governments to commit themselves to meet the basic needs of their people? This is not a problem unique to a basic needs approach, for all approaches to helping the poor face this. How do we get LDC governments to provide employment for the poor or to redistribute income to the poor? If all external assistance were tied to a basic needs approach, there would at least be some incentive to undertake such services. Nonetheless, this is a difficult political question and will be decided in each country. At the very least foreign assistance donors should not assist LDC governments that have not made a commitment to basic needs provision.

Measuring Performance

How do we measure performance in meeting basic needs? This is extremely difficult. LDC governments put up fences around their poverty. They don't want outsiders to see the extent of income inequality, hunger, squalor, disease, etc.

William McGreevey has laid out the issues in measuring LDC performance in Annex D to USAID, *Socio-Economic Performance Criteria for Development*, 1977. The Overseas Development Council has made a start toward measuring performance in the Physical Quality of Life Index (measuring infant mortality rates, life expectancy, and literacy) which has been published in *Agenda, 1977*.

A Satisfaction of Basic Needs Index (SBNI) has been developed by John Richardson and Eloise Forgette. This index measures national performance, relative to needs, in the areas of nutrition, medical services, housing, and employment. Data have been collected for 20 nations for the period 1950 to 1976.

Role of Foreign Assistance

What is the role for foreign assistance in meeting basic needs? Actually, USAID has been moving in this direction since the passage of the Foreign Assistance Act of 1973 and the World Bank and other foreign assistance agencies are considering meeting basic needs as the target for development.

Foreign assistance donors can make it clear that they will only assist LDC governments committed to meeting basic needs. They can help LDCs identify people living in poverty, help determine their priority needs, provide technical assistance and training in alternative delivery systems for meeting needs and can provide resources on a declining basis to fund the programs to meet basic needs.

The OEEC was set up jointly by the U.S. and Europe to allocate Marshall Plan funds and to measure performance in using those funds. Perhaps a similar organization could be set up in connection with a basic needs strategy.

Mobilizing People for Self-Reliance

The third strategy at the national level is a strategy to mobilize people for self-reliance. The only way people can meet their basic needs is if they do it themselves. There is no way the World Bank of AID or the national governments of the poor countries can provide people with housing, food, clothing, medical care, etc. This would be a global welfare scheme and would fail. Thus, the fundamental strategy to meet basic needs must be to mobilize people to meet their own needs. This involves providing catalytic agents. We must analyze what functions can be centralized and which must be decentralized, which needs can be met privately and which must be met publicly. In the barefoot doctor scheme in China (often cited as an example of a solution to the basic needs for medical care) some of the functions were centralized, some were decentralized. There was a national strategy to provide barefoot doctors. Training centers were established. However, each village chose its own candidate for training, each village paid its own barefoot doctor, etc. There was a combination of centralization and decentralization.

Sri Lanka has apparently developed a fairly effective program for organizing people at the local level. These local level organizations—with the assistance of the government—then meet the basic needs of their members.

The starting point in meeting basic needs must be the acceptance and encouragement of indigenous efforts to solve the problem. But the economic problem cannot be seen in isolation, it must be realized that indigenous solutions will of necessity grow out of the political process in each country. The effort to transmit Western solutions has all too often resulted in the creation or acceptance of authoritarian and repressive regimes which were seen as able to foster growth. By their nature these regimes inhibit the political invention, social innovation, and economic problem solving which are at the core of self-generating efforts at development. Political activity is the source of cultural creativity. LDCs cannot borrow blueprints from the outside, they cannot get technical solutions from the outside, they cannot adopt strategies from the outside. Technocrats cannot solve the problem.

Human rights and political participation are thus instrumental variables, as well as ends in themselves, if authentic models of development are to emerge in the LDCs. Third World solutions to their own problems require political activity, debate, controversy, confrontation, experiments, trial and error.

The basic needs focus is an intensely political approach to development. The poverty problem can only be solved through politics, as is obviously true in the United States. The 1960s War on Poverty was a political process, and dealing with the poverty problem is a political process in every country.

One reason the poor stay so poor is that they have no political clout—no role in the politics of the society. To bring them out of poverty requires politicization of the poor and their active involvement in community action.

Educational systems must be restructured to provide for critical self-awareness. People must come to realize that there are alternatives to the status quo, that there are different ways of doing things, that they can do things for themselves.

This is obviously a very risky business for governments. Our own experience with the Community Action Programs of the War on Poverty taught us that much can be learned from this U.S. experience as well as from successes and failures in LDCs.

International Level

The final component of a reformist strategy to meet basic needs is a call to restructure the international economic order. Mahbub ul Haq has made this case in *The Third World and the International Economic Order*. Haq argues that if we are going to have growth with equity, not only do we have to restructure the domestic economy, we also have to restructure the international economy, and it is here that the economic and political changes will most affect the U.S. It is not just a Third World problem but is a world problem.

The existing international economic order favors increasing inequalities between countries and increasing social imbalance within LDCs. These are linked phenomena. During the last 25 years per capita income more than doubled in the world, but it was concentrated in the hands of the developed countries and the privileged in LDCs.

What policy should be followed in re-shaping the IEO? First, a redistribution of international credit is needed. Today 70% of the world's population in LDCs get 4% of the international liquidity (SDRs) created in the IMF, but this formula must be altered to channel more international credit to LDCs in the future so that they can make it on their own. An analogy can be made to programs in the U.S. to channel credit to small farmers (the Farmer's Home Administration) or small business (the Small Business Administration). The same principle should be applied internationally.

International financial and technical assistance should encourage LDCs to process, transport, insure, and distribute their own products. At the present time, LDCs get $30 billion each year for their exports which are sold in the developed countries for $200 billion. The $170 billion difference goes to the middleman who processes, ships, transports, insures, and distributes these goods in the developed countries. If more of these services were provided by less expensive labor in LDCs, not only would the value-added in LDCs rise, but the final price paid by the consumer in developed countries might actually fall.

Developed countries should move vigorously to reduce tariffs and quotas on labor intensive goods which can be produced much more cheaply in LDCs. Again, this results in increased income in LDCs and lower prices for consumers in developed countries. The problems of course come from the dislocation caused the workers in affected industries. Developed country governments must take an active role in assisting these industries.

Developed countries should greatly increase the amount of foreign assistance going to LDCs. This foreign assistance should be seen as an obligation—not as an act of charity. In this regard they should support moves toward some form of international taxation, e.g., on the seabeds, non-renewable resources, etc. The revenue generated from international taxation should clearly go to those governments which have committed themselves to meeting the basic needs of their citizens.

Developed countries should accept a larger role for the LDCs in international economic decision-making. At the present time, 70% of the world's population lives in LDCs and has less than one-third of the votes in the IMF and IBRD. A larger voice for the LDCs is clearly in order—commensurate with their increasing importance in the international economy.

With these changes, Haq sees the international sphere coming to play a more positive role in development and one which may actually facilitate growth and equity.

III
SUMMARY AND CONCLUSIONS

We are witnessing a profound shift in perception concerning the meaning of development. A consensus is emerging that the goal of development is to meet basic needs.

There are no satisfactory data on the dimensions of poverty and deprivation in the world. The UN Conferences on Food, Habitat, Water, etc., have begun the process of estimating global needs for food, water, shelter, health care, and education. The World Bank staff has assembled those very tentative data and made some very preliminary estimates of the investment, recurrent, and total costs of meeting these needs using alternative approaches. Foreign assistance components of such a strategy have also been estimated.

All these estimates are quite arbitrary and based on little hard data. However, the effort, despite the limitations, is commendable. It was only after the U.S. population and leadership became aware of the dimensions of domestic poverty that an effort was launched to deal with that poverty. The effort has had mixed results but there has been some success. But the data on poverty amidst affluence had to be generated first.

There is no consensus concerning the appropriate strategy for meeting basic needs. The old consensus on a capital oriented strategy of development has been shattered and development theory is currently in a state of disarray and confusion.

The revolutionaries are pushing for massive social, political and economic transformation as a pre-condition for meeting basic needs. They are optimistic concerning the chances of success based largely on the example of China.

Reformists have been forced to come up with an alternative to the now discredited traditional and the politically unacceptable revolutionary strategies. The alternative is a strategy emphasizing growth with equity.

The growth with equity strategies call for both rural and urban developments that will benefit the poor. These development strategies emphasize increasing productivity and incomes; meeting basic needs directly; and mobilization for self reliance. Various theorists push for employment generating technologies, redirecting investment to increase productivity of the poor, and human resource development. At the international level, a new international economic order is deemed necessary if basic needs are to be met.

The developing countries and the development community are caught up in an exciting and possibly fruitful debate from which the poor of the world may benefit. Their basic needs may be met in part as the result of new development and development assistance strategies.

BIBLIOGRAPHY

Adelman, I. and Morris, C. T., *Economic Growth and Social Equity in Developing Countries* (Stanford, 1973).

Adelman, I., "Growth, Income Distribution, and Equity Oriented Development Strategies," *World Development* 3 #2-3 (February-March 1975).

Burki, Shahid Jared and Voorhoero, Joris, *Global Estimates for Meeting Basic Needs: Background Paper*, Washington: World Bank Basic Needs Paper No. 1, 1977.

Burki, S. J., Hicks, Norman, and Haq. Mahbub, *Pakistan: Operational Implications of Adopting Basic Needs Targets*, Washington: World Bank Basic Needs Paper No. 4, 1977.

Chenery, H., et al., *Redistribution with Growth* (Oxford, 1974).

Grant, J., "A Fresh Approach to Meeting Basic Human Needs of the World's Poorest Billion: Implications of the Chinese and Other 'Success Models,' " *American Political Science Association* (1976).

Griffin, K., *The Political Economy of Agrarian Change* (London: Macmillan, 1974).

Gurley, J., "Rural Development in China 1949–72, and the Lessons to be Learned from It," *World Development* 3 #7-8 (July-August 1975), pp. 455–471.

Haq, M., *The Poverty Curtain* (New York: Columbia University Press, 1976).

Haq, Mahbub, *Basic Needs: A Progress Report,* Washington: World Bank, 1977.

Johnston, Bruce and Kilby, Peter, *Agriculture and Structural Transformation* (New York: Oxford University Press, 1975).

Liedholm, C., Byerlee, D., Eicher, C. K., Spencer, D. S. C., *Rural Employment in Tropical Africa: Summary of Findings* (East Lansing: Michigan State University, 1977).

McGreevey, W. P., "Issues in Measuring Development Performance," in *Socio-Economic Performance Criteria for Development* (AID, 1977).

Mellor, J., *The New Economics of Growth* (Cornell, 1976).

Morawetz, David, *Twenty-Five Years of Economic Development,* Washington: World Bank, 1977.

ODC (Overseas Development Council), *Agenda for Action, 1977* (Washington, 1977).

Pack, H., "The Employment-Output Trade-Off in LDCs—A Micro-Economic Approach," *Oxford Economic Papers* (November 1974).

Ranis, G., "Equity With Growth in Taiwan: How 'Special' is the 'Special Case'?" (New Haven: Yale, 1977).

Richardson, John M. and Forgette, Eloise, *The Satisfaction of Basic Human Needs Index* (Washington: American University Center for Technology and Administration, 1977).

Schumacher, E. F., *Small is Beautiful* (New York: Harper and Row, 1973).

Simmons, John and Phillips, Tony, *Education for Basic Human Needs,* Washington: World Bank, 1977.

Streeten, Paul and Haq, Mahbub, *International Implications for Donor Countries and Agencies of Meeting Basic Human Needs,* Washington: World Bank Basic Needs Paper No. 3, 1977.

Streeten, Paul, *The Distinctive Features of a Basic Needs Approach to Development,* Washington: World Bank Basic Needs Paper No. 2, 1977.

Waterston, A., "A Viable Model for Rural Development," *Finance and Development* (December 1974, and March 1975).

Wells, Louis T., "Economic Man and Engineering Man: Choice of Technology in a Low Wage Country," *Harvard Development Research Group Report No. 226* (November 1972).

Strategies for Meeting Human Needs

Denis Goulet

An ancient saying warns that: "When the gods decide to punish their enemies, they grant them all their wishes." These words might well be inscribed on the office walls of those development planners who speak as though all human needs could be met if only the right strategy were found. Yet anthropologist Dorothy Lee correctly notes:

> It is value, not a series of needs, which is at the basis of human behavior. The main difference between the two lies in the conception of the good which underlies them. The premise that man acts so as to satisfy needs presupposes a negative conception of the good as amelioration or the correction of an undesirable state. According to this view, man acts to relieve tension; good is the removal of evil and welfare the correction of ills; satisfaction is the meeting of a need; good functioning comes from adjustment, survival from adaptation; peace is the resolution of conflict; fear, of the supernatural or of adverse public opinion, is the incentive to good conduct; the happy individual is the well-adjusted individual.[1]

In conclusion, Lee writes: "If there are needs, they are derivative not basic. If, for example, physical survival was held as the ultimate goal in some society, it would probably be found to give rise to those needs which have been stated to be basic to human survival; but I know of no culture where human physical survival has been shown, rather than unquestioningly assumed by social scientists, to be the ultimate goal."[2] The most basic question, therefore, is not: "What are one's needs?" But rather, "What are one's values, and what does one need to achieve them?" New evidence that values determine needs, and not the inverse, came to

47

light in 1971 with the dramatic discovery of the Tasaday Stone Age tribes in Southern Mindanao, an island of the Philippines. As one writer describes the Tasaday:

> Their outstanding characteristic is a complete lack of aggressiveness. They have no word for weapon, hostility, anger, or war. . . . All of the food they collect (yams, fruit, berries, flowers, fish, crabs, frogs) they divide equally with scrupulous care among all members of the band. They are curious about objects from the outside world, but they are not acquisitive. After examining such objects carefully they will return them, saying, "Thank you, we finished looking." . . . Living in a benevolent environment, with all of their needs satisfied by the resources of their food-gathering area of 25 square kilometers, they have no external enemies, and they have existed for centuries in complete peace with one another. In the words of a Filipino anthropologist, the Tasaday can help us identify "the qualities of humanity, the so-called universals which all men share . . . to better understand ourselves and the problems we have created. . . . We will never know how much we have gained until we learn how much we have lost."[3]

The risk of ethnocentrism and bias is inherent in any attempt to analyze fundamental human needs. Indeed needs themselves, however basic they may appear to development scholars or practitioners, are defined as needs relative to other goods. A discussion of need strategies, therefore, should take as its primary task, not spelling out measures for meeting needs, but rather asking prior questions about how to think about needs. This is the path the present essay follows: first, a series of questions will be posed regarding how one may think about needs. Only afterward will problems faced by various possible need strategies be examined.

I
PRIOR QUESTIONS, DIFFICULT CERTITUDES, AND COMPETING NEED THEORIES

"One man's meat is another man's poison." This proverb dramatizes the relativities inherent in desires, tastes, preferences, and needs. Yet, although physical survival "at any cost" may not be a cherished value of any society, as Lee claims, it remains true nonetheless that survival is a highly cherished value for all. And there is some justification for initially asking: What goods are needed for survival? The correlative question is, evidently: What goods or values are considered more noble or worthy than survival? Here as elsewhere ethnocentrism rears its ugly, and omnipresent, head. The high indices of suicide in "developed" countries have often blinded observers to the truth that material sufficiency, or abundance, may be less essential—even for survival—than is the presence of *meaning*. In order to survive one must want to survive, but how can one want to survive unless life has a meaning? Accordingly, having a meaningful existence may well be the most basic of all human needs. Food itself, so obviously essential for physical subsistence, ceases to be desirable in circumstances where life loses its attractiveness. I myself have witnessed[4] the refusal to eat proffered food on the part of resigned aged members of societies whose continued presence in a semi-nomadic community ceased to have meaning once their functional utility had waned.[5] In a similar vein, Piers Paul Read tells of the paralyzing revulsion experienced by certain passengers of a crashed plane toward eating the flesh of their deceased fellows[6] even when the only alternative was quick starvation. These cases, admittedly extreme, shed light on our reflection regarding more "normal" attitudes toward allegedly basic needs. A sense of esteem, especially self-esteem or dignity, and of meaningful self-identity appear to be closely intertwined as primordial pillars of human need. Because this is so, one laments seeing so many contemporary writings[7] limit their examination of human needs almost exclusively to purely physiological, sociological, or psychological needs. This emphasis is dictated in large measure by two considerations: first, physical needs are more easily measured by quantitative instruments in use; and second, the satisfaction of such needs is presumed to be required before other needs can be met. This last assumption runs throughout Maslow's writings on human needs.[8] Maslow argues that higher needs appear after lower-level satisfactions have been attained. In real life, however, no such artificial boundaries can be found. Even the poorest societies—and the poorest local communities—devote some of their meager resources to satisfying needs of a higher, symbolic, spiritual or communal order—"gratuity" needs, as it were! This is clearly the case of slum-dwellers in Brazil's teeming cities who borrow and pawn so as to give themselves a few days of cathartic fantasy as "king, pirate, or mythical hero" during the revelry of Carnival season. Michael Harrington is simply the latest in a long line of Western social critics who, upon visiting India, note with an astonished sense of discovery that rich cultural manifestations can co-exist alongside the most shocking levels of material poverty. Harrington writes:

> Even if there are enormous relativities to be faced here, and even though I will not understand most of them, there are some absolutes too. Dying is one—infant mortality, early death. Disease and twisted limbs are others. One of the defenses the affluent Westerner builds in the presence of a country like India is the myth of its exotic holiness. "They" must like to live at low levels of consumption and energy; we must not disturb the culture they have built out of their suffering and misery. That is true in part, and nonsense in part, pernicious nonsense. Yes, a people who make a culture out of their limitations, out of their deaths and famines, have thereby asserted their freedom and transcended those limits by the very fact of having been able to turn them into symbols. Malraux said that well in *The Voices of Silence*. He understood that the culture evoked by a cruel existence was not itself cruel, but the release from cruelty, its sublimation. But all that is justified only so long as it is inevitable. To honor the stoic acceptance of the death of babies in an age when medicine might save them is criminal, not cultural.[9]

Three relevant points stand out in this text, none of which can be omitted in any critical reflection on need satisfaction. (1) Even in the face of all relativities traceable to culture, history, or geography, certain *physical* evils are intolerable. (2) The satisfaction of higher needs, at a societal, cultural, and spiritual level is possible in spite of great poverty, perhaps even because of it. (This is what Maslow and other Westerners often overlook, thanks to their implicit assumption that material well-being and technological modernity are synonymous with high civilization.) (3) Cultural achievements of a high order are no excuse for leaving physical needs unsatisfied when it is possible to do so.

I shall not repeat here the analysis presented in an earlier work on the survival strategy or "existence rationality" any society deploys in its quest for survival, meaning, and identity.[10] Existence rationality, it will be recalled, is "the *process* by which a society devises a conscious strategy for obtaining its goals, given its ability to process information and the constraints weighing upon it." In the modern world it is now possible, even in societies whose patterns of life are themselves not modern, to absorb and process much more information than ever before about technological possibilities. More importantly, it is possible to remove some of the constraints weighing upon them. This is the reason why, as Harrington argues, "cruel existence is justified only so long as it is inevitable." The point is not that physical evils are absolutes; they remain, in Dorothy Lee's terms, relative. But they become absolutely intolerable once they are no longer inevitable.

Accordingly, the key developmental question is how to meet certain categories of physical needs without imposing staggering costs in human sufferings and cultural destruction.[11] Neither stagnation in mass poverty nor growth at all costs is to be uncritically endorsed: both are highly destructive of central human values. No facile optimism is warranted, for as Hobart Rowen, an experienced journalist, recently noted: "Economic-development strategy as pursued for the last 25 years has failed to reduce poverty in India or to increase the standard of living. World Bank data suggest, as a matter of fact, that a large percentage of the rural population is worse off than it was 15 years ago."[12]

The French personalist philosopher Emmanuel Mounier entitled one of his books *The Difficult Certitudes*. Our own certitudes on this question are also difficult. It is certain that needs must be met; it is certain that they have not been adequately met by approaches tried thus far; it is certain that new strategies must be devised; and it is no less certain that these will not necessarily prove better able to succeed than their predecessors. Little of *strategic* value is gained by drawing up new lists of needs, or by classifying them in some slightly different way than before. It is evident that in some sense all human beings are capable of aspiring to, and therefore of needing, such varied goods as: life-sustenance, emotional and physical comfort, esteem, freedom, community, love, participation, security, fulfillment, peace, order, meaning, mystery, and transcendence. There is very little, however, that a properly developmental strategy can do in the face of this litany of needs, except to heed Keynes' admonition that economists are the "trustees not of civilization, but of the possibility of civilization."[13] Galbraith is correct in suggesting that the "final requirement of modern development planning is that it have a theory of consumption . . . a view of what the production is ultimately for."[14]

What production is for is the provision of essential goods and services to those who most badly need them. But who can say which goods will be produced, and for whom, unless we examine the incentive systems to which productive energies respond in given societies.

Incentive Systems

Theories of human need drawn from personal speculation or group model-building abound. One has only to evoke names like Herbert Marcuse or Norman Brown (with their theory of "eroticizing" material needs in non-repressive fashion), of David McClelland (for whom the drive to achieve which exists differentially in individuals ought to dictate social change strategies), Garrett Hardin (who preaches the urgency of practicing "triage" in order to sort out, from among the globe's poor, those who can "viably" be lifted up to "responsible affluence"), Erich Fromm (who fears that most people prefer to have their needs paternalistically met by others so that they can "escape from freedom"), and the world modelers (Harlan Cleveland, Ervin Laszlo, the Club of Rome, Herman Kahn, the Bariloche Group, John and Magada McHale, et al.) to perceive how vast is the gamut of need theories. Perhaps the most intriguing contemporary need theorist is Ivan Illich, who preaches an "iron law" of need pre-emption, according to which packagers with a vested interest in providing certain goods pre-empt the social legitimacy surrounding "generic" needs and redefine them to match the "specific" goods they themselves provide. Illich charges schools with doing this to meet the hunger for knowledge; hospitals and doctors to profit from the desire all people have to enjoy good health; and automobile manufacturers to translate locomotion needs to a need for cars.[15] The central questions remain the same: By whom are needs decided, and in response to which incentives?

One must answer by analyzing overall incentive systems at work in any society. Certain needs are determined simply by the dictates of nature and biology, although one should not too hastily conclude that quantified minimum intakes of calories and proteins are as invariable as some official reports purport them to be. Some needs are also dictated by the arbiters of culture. In more recent times, tribal, peasant, and so-called "transitional" societies have fallen prey to having their needs defined by a succession of extrinsically induced "demonstration effects" leading to what Daniel Lerner long ago[16] designated as "psychic mobility" or the capacity to imagine another way of living. Also important as a source of new desires or needs[17] is the emergence of new ones from below as individuals and groups gain additional purchasing power or greater technical capacities to create new wealth. Probably the main creator of new needs, however, is the political process of attacking what Marx termed the "false consciousness" of the exploited which leads them to think that deprivation is a "natural" phenomenon. Such ideological "conscientization" attributes, on the contrary, much deprivation to a process of unjust appropriation of scarce goods by dominant classes or interest groups. Once the poor understood, therefore, that the curtailment of their desires constitutes the internalization of someone else's dominant, and domineering values, new needs emerge in them.

In most less-developed countries, all of these fonts of need-creation are simultaneously at work. The net result is that the poor demand more goods and, concomitantly, an increasing number of the rich likewise advocate providing at least a "sufficiency" of goods to the neediest. This the rich do for many reasons: in order to expand the markets of sellers, so as to satisfy certain ideals of social justice and redistributive equity, in order to dilute dangers of explosive revolution, and to allay guilt feelings over shocking inequalities in goods. Not surprisingly, therefore, even "conventional" development agencies such as the World Bank, the United Nations, the Organization for Economic Co-operation and Development and the U.S. Agency for International Development now preach the merits of a strategy which places high priority on meeting the basic needs of the poor.[18] They emphasize abolishing absolute poverty by a direct assault instead of trying to promote aggregate economic growth whose benefits will then "trickle down" to the poor. Strategists of the basic needs school likewise contend that income and wealth gaps are so wide that it is "unrealistic" to devise development strategies aimed at reducing these gaps. Consequently, they exhibit little concern for relative deprivation. Yet, here lies a problem which, along with several others, calls for further comment.

II

PROBLEMS IN BASIC NEEDS STRATEGIES

The component elements of a Basic Needs Development Strategy (BN) are well-known to students of the question. But serious problems abide, not only in conflicts over definitions, measurement, and priorities but also in the relative position to be assigned to resource allocations aimed at meeting basic needs and others having other objectives. As the British economist Paul Streeten does well to note,[19] there are two competing ways of defining a BN approach to development. The first is to treat BN as an all-embracing and exclusive development strategy. This definition of BN embraces the major components of previous efforts:

rural development, urban poverty alleviation, employment creation, redistribution with growth, etc. Although this conception may appeal to a wide constituency under a large banner, Streeten judges it to be politically unrealistic and intellectually clumsy, suffering as it does from fuzzy demarcation lines. He prefers the second approach which treats BN as a strategy which supplements and complements existing strategies. A BN strategy places high priority on meeting specified needs of the poorest people, not primarily to raise productivity but as an end in itself. Drawing on the experience of The People's Republic of China and other societies, it declares its objectives to be feasible. It calls for a strong dose of what Streeten calls "supply management" so that increases in the incomes of the poor are not neutralized by increases in the prices of the goods and services on which they spend these increments. A substantial government role is postulated because the neediest people can influence markets only marginally with their buying power. Most importantly, BN strategies stress several non-material goods: specifically, self-reliance, local participation, freedom of choice at the grass-roots, employment that is culturally meaningful, and the like. Finally, such strategies attempt to quantify the resources needed to meet targets, while simultaneously measuring a wide range of social gains.[20] Resource requirements are estimated both domestically and internationally. A host of conceptual and operational problems clearly need to be solved if BN strategies are to become working tools of governments, international agencies, and private organizations seeking to promote development. Above all else, the ideas circulating in development arenas must correspond to the aspirations of grass-roots communities of human need. Several knotty conceptual problems demand comment.

Resource Scarcity and Self-Reliance

Most advocates of BN also seek to promote self-reliance and to elicit change which builds from within the latent dynamism of indigenous values. Inevitably they face the problem described by political scientist Robert Packenham as the myth that "all good things come together."[21] In real conditions of under-development, however, cherished values such as self-reliance and meeting basic needs often pull societies in opposite directions. This is especially true where resources are extremely scarce.[22] In conditions of dire poverty, rapid improvement in satisfying basic needs may require a considerable inpouring of resources from outside sources. Too much "aid," however, may easily undermine efforts to achieve self-reliance. Special pedagogies may doubtless be employed to use aid to help people become more self-reliant,[23] but success is certainly not assured and, of itself, dependence on external assistance tends to reduce self-reliance. Self-reliance is clearly not synonymous with self-sufficiency or autarchy. Nonetheless, there are powerful overtones of what Latin Americans call "assistentialism"[24] in a BN strategy preached too unidimensionally.

Needs Versus Demands

It is easy for the stewards of development models to formulate a "basic needs strategy" which would, in effect, merely constitute a disguised form of class exploitation, treating "the poorest billion," as it were, as the world's basket cases or mere welfare recipients. Therefore, the true requirement is for a strategy *to meet needs in ways which empower the poor to make effective demands on the social systems within which they live.* These systems are complex, however, and multiple, ranging from myriad varieties of local "patron" systems to international trade arrangements which, in the words of Gunnar Myrdal, had the purpose of *"explaining away the international equality problem."*[25]

The real danger lies in that too exclusive a concern for the abolition of absolute poverty can easily lend legitimacy to societal systems—local, regional, national, and international—in which glaring disparities in wealth, status, effective influence, and power are accepted as unimportant, all in the name of meeting basic needs. The issue of relative poverty must also be faced directly. This is not to argue, of course, that the abolition of absolute poverty is not important or does not constitute a first claim on resource allocations. But any *comprehensive* development strategy must utilize its very address of absolute poverty as a means of relative empowerment of the poorest so that they are effectively "capacitated" to make demands on their surrounding environments—social, economic, and political—which will also launch them dynamically on a trajectory of improvement of their *relative* position. In the language of social discourse conducted within the United States, the debate is between those who contend that it suffices to provide equality of opportunity to the disadvantaged and those who argue that at least some basic equality of results or of outcome must be guaranteed by policy.[26]

A parallel debate around Third World development strategies contrasts theories (and strategies) which stress the centrality of *resource transfers* with those which, without denying the need for such transfers, give primacy to new ground rules for the *distribution of power*. It may well be necessary, for tactical reasons, to concentrate efforts for a time on building consensus around the abolition, or drastic reduction, of absolute poverty in the world by the year 2000. But this objective can never substitute for the restructuring of the International Economic Order (IEO)[27] in ways which will alter relative patterns of poverty as well. Similarly, national policies of "meeting basic needs" cannot replace, but should complement, policies of creating overall incentive systems which are more equitable and socially just.

In short, one principal reason why absolute poverty is so intolerable is that it co-exists alongside relative deprivations which dramatize the injustice and dysfunctionality of most societal systems of economic rewards and penalties. A sound basic needs strategy must therefore aim at integrating special efforts to abolish absolute misery with dynamic, processional steps to reduce relative disparities. This means that any new global compact must approach the poverty problem from two directions simultaneously. From below, there must be a "bottom threshold" of minimum goods provided to all on the basis of need. And from above, movement is required in the direction of assuring that resources are not diverted to wasteful, luxurious, or unnecessary uses. Floors and ceilings to resource use are equally necessary.[28]

Conflicting Needs and Priorities

Under conditions of scarcity it is impossible to satisfy all needs adequately. As Arthur Okun does well to remind us, there are always painful trade-offs to be made between competing values and needs.[29] At times the price paid for full employment in the Third World is lesser productivity and more modest levels of material satisfactions *for all*. Mao was fond of describing true austerity as the "strenuous striving after a decent sufficiency for all." Many societies will doubtless have to learn the painful lesson that they "can't have their cake and eat it." That is, if they seek military power and prestigious technology, they cannot have consumer abundance. Or if they seek competitive industry, they cannot also have highly self-sufficient agriculture, if only because they possess limited resources with which to build requisite infrastructures. At the height of the Vietnam War, Lyndon Johnson took it for granted that Americans could afford both "guns and butter." As it turned out, the poorer categories of Americans could afford neither. The point is that any veritable need *strategy* must establish hierarchies and priorities in needs. Since its coup in 1973, the Chilean military junta has placed greater importance on lowering inflation and rendering Chile's monetary position internationally more competitive than on providing jobs or essential services to its poor masses. Its choices reveal what its true priorities are.

Similarly, basic needs strategists need to lay bare what their priorities are. They cannot simply assume that, in very poor countries, there will be enough to satisfy everyone's basic needs all at once: Will nutritional needs come first, or health services, or educational opportunities? In addition, whatever may be one's preference for investing in "developmental" projects, natural catastrophes—floods, hurricanes, typhoons, droughts, and earthquakes—come along unexpectedly to divert scarce funds for emergency relief uses. Speaking concretely, there is great merit in the advocacy by Lappé and Collins, co-authors of the seminal *Food First*, of food self-sufficiency in every third world country.[30] In many places, however, the investments needed to render local agricultural structures more productive will pre-empt all possibilities of providing basic health services for the needy rural masses, or new educational opportunities to them. Hence "food first" can never come to mean "food only." Yet as soon as one says food *first*, one says health or housing, or some other basic need *second*. My point is simply to recall that even good strategies entail social costs and sacrificed priorities.

III
CONCLUSION

The essential argument of this paper is that a basic needs strategy for a locality, region, nation, or the world itself can only be derived from certain main values. One of these values holds that all humans must "have" enough in order to "be" fully human. One derivative conclusion states that the many can only have *enough* if societies so organize themselves that the *few* cannot have too much. As Erich Fromm pointed out, "affluent alienation" is no less dehumanizing than "impoverished alienation."[31] To reach a new kind of social contract or "global bargain" regarding resource use which renders sufficiency of goods possible to all will require what one corporate planner calls a "deep mutation." In the words of Dutch economist André van Dam of the Corn Products Corporation:

> Global development may be defined as the process of man's legitimate aspiration to the basic amenities of life with a minimum inequity in their distribution. This is a long and deep mutation, that comes inevitably at a price: change into the unknown, perhaps accelerated change in the beginning.[32]

Another central value, from which a specification of needs is to be derived, is the quest for meaningfulness in life. Any mode of satisfying material needs which strips people of their identity, their cultural integrity, their belief systems, or the meanings they attach to existence cannot be sound. A comprehensive basic needs strategy recognizes that *how* needs are met is no less important than *that* they be met. The poor must obtain new resources in ways which transform them into creators, and not mere consumers, of civilization. Thus any imagery which portrays the poorest billion or the bottom 40% as welfare recipients is unsatisfactory.

Finally, one must assure that the social sacrifices attendant upon abolishing absolute poverty are borne primarily by those who can bear them. Consequently, the relatively favored classes will have to accept new ground rules of access to resources early in the sequence of decisions about their ultimate use. Elsewhere I have called this the principle of resource access upstream, instead of downstream.[33] Obviously, if the world's poor can only make claims on resources after goods have been appropriated and processed by the rich, the best they can hope for is some palliative welfare system. On the other hand, the full panoply of their basic needs—for dignity, for effective participation in shaping their social destinies, for the esteem that comes to those who are self-reliant—can best be met if they can make effective demands on the economic incentive systems operative in their societies.

The interest now displayed by development specialists in "basic needs strategies" reflects a desire on the part of many to find new patterns of resource transfers.[34] More significantly, many social commentators now search for fresh approaches to development itself and to living styles within rich countries.[35] This search needs to be enriched, I think, by more explicitly linking the preferred values of any society to its chosen development strategies, and to the criteria it employs for defining and meeting fundamental needs. A *vital nexus*[36] of the three must serve as the articulating principle of strategies designed to lead to a form of development that is good for the people and not merely for the statisticians. I am here paraphrasing the statement made by General Garrastazu-Medici, then president of Brazil, that his country's economic miracle was "good for the economy, but bad for the people."

No serious development theorist or practitioner dares to preach the merits of a form of development which is not good, that is, directly beneficial to "the people" and more specifically, the poorest people. Cynics and skeptics will doubtless retort, as did La Rochefoucauld before them, that "ideals are just the hypocritical tribute which vice renders to virtue." In truth much rhetoric around "basic needs strategies" may well mask new rationalizations for business as usual, or for the "trickle down" of benefits to the poor without altering the underlying bases of re-source use. Nevertheless, the present global intellectual climate is ready for truly creative new approaches to basic needs.

The purpose of this paper has been to satisfy one basic human need, namely, that of demystifying the confusion surrounding most contemporary discussions of the matter. Clarity of discourse and realism of analysis are basic needs felt by all who would work on behalf of authentic development.

NOTES

1. Dorothy D. Lee, "Are Basic Needs Ultimate?" in *Freedom and Culture: Essays* (Englewood Cliffs, N.J.: Prentice-Hall, 1959), p. 72.

2. *Ibid.*

3. L. S. Stavrianos, *The Promise of The Coming Dark Age* (San Francisco: W. H. Freeman and Company, 1976).

4. In the territory of Rondonia, Brazil in 1961, while living with Paacas Novos Indians.

5. A much more dramatic case is described at length by Colin M. Turnbull in *The Mountain People* (New York: Simon and Schuster, 1972).

6. *Cf.* Piers Paul Read, *Alive* (New York: Avon Books, 1975).

7. I shall not attempt to present a detailed bibliography of such writings. Readers may consult such works as: *Employment, Growth and Basic Needs: A One-World Problem*, prepared by the International Labor Office (New York: Praeger, 1977); *The Planetary Bargain, Proposals for a New International Economic Order to Meet Human Needs*, Aspen Institute for Humanistic Studies (Aspen, Colorado); Report of a Workshop held July 7–August 1, 1975; John and Magda Cordell McHale, *Human Requirements, Supply Levels and Other Bounds: A Framework for Thinking About the Planetary Bargain* (Aspen Institute, 1975); Jan Tinbergen, ed., *RIO: Reshaping the International Order* (New York: E. P. Dutton, 1976); Amilcar O. Herrera, *et al.*, *Catastrophe or New Society? A Latin American World Model* (Ottawa: International Development Research Centre, 1976); Ervin Laszlo, *et al.*, *Goals for Mankind* (New York: E. P. Dutton, 1977). Also worth examining are several unpublished papers, notably: James P. Grant and John W. Sewell, "Basic Human Needs and the New International Economic Order; A Northern View," November 1977, 28 pp.; Danny M. Leipziger and Maureen A. Lewis, "A Basic Needs Approach to Development," September 1977, 34 pp.; Paul Streeten, "Basic Needs: An Issues Paper," March 1977, 21 pp.; Mahbub Ul Haq, "Basic Needs: A Progress Report," August 1977, 10 pp.; Firouz Vakil, "Basic

Human Needs and the Growth Process: The Dimensions of the Conflict," June 1977, 41 pp. On differing perceptions of needs, see George H. Gallup, "Human Needs and Satisfactions: A Global Survey," *Public Opinion Quarterly*, Vol. 40 (1976), pp. 459–467.

8. Cf. Abraham H. Maslow, ed. *New Knowledge in Human Values* (New York: Harper and Row, 1959); Maslow, *Toward a Psychology of Being*, 2nd ed. (New York: Van Nostrand Reinhold, 1968); Maslow, ed., *Motivation and Personality*, 2nd ed. (New York: Harper and Row, 1970); and Maslow, *Farther Reaches of Human Nature* (New York: Viking Press, 1971).

9. Michael Harrington, *The Vast Majority, A Journey to the World's Poor* (New York: Simon and Schuster, 1977), p. 61.

10. Denis Goulet, *The Cruel Choice* (New York: Atheneum, 1971), pp. 187–214.

11. On this see Peter L. Berger, *Pyramids of Sacrifice, Political Ethics and Social Change* (New York: Basic Books, 1974). For a critique of this book see Denis Goulet, "Pyramids of Sacrifice, The High Price of Social Change," *Christianity and Crisis*, Vol. 35 No. 16 (October 13, 1975), pp. 231–237.

12. Hobart Rowen, "India's Only Hope," *The Washington Post*, Thursday, December 1, 1977, p. A 17.

13. Cited in Benjamin Higgins, *Economic Development, Problems, Principles, & Policies*, Revised Edition (New York: W. W. Norton & Co., 1968). p. 3.

14. John Kenneth Galbraith, *Economic Development in Perspective* (Cambridge, Mass.: Harvard University Press, 1962), p. 43.

15. Ivan Illich, *Deschooling Society* (New York: Harper and Row, 1971); *idem, Medical Nemesis: The Expropriation of Health* (New York: Pantheon, 1976); and *Energy and Equity* (New York: Harper and Row, 1974).

16. In *The Passing of Traditional Society* (New York: The Free Press, 1958), p. 52. For Lerner's more recent views, cf. Khosrow Jahandary, "Modernization Revisited: An Interview with Daniel Lerner," *Communications and Development Review*, Vol. 1 Nos. 2, 3 (Summer–Autumn 1977), pp. 4–6.

17. In this context no attempt is made to differentiate, as many theorists do, between needs and desires. Once either is effectively expressed as a *demand*, it creates identical pressures on social systems, economic and political. Consequently, for strategic purposes, they are equivalent. Nevertheless, it is obvious that decision-makers must establish priorities in accord with some criteria which distinguishes needs from desires. For one instructive analysis of the difference between the two, see Mario Kamenetsky, *Economia del Conocimiento y Empresa* (Buenos Aires: Editorial Paidos, 1976), pp. 22–26.

18. One recent statement of the approach is found in James P. Grant, "The Poorest Billion People: A New Approach to Basic Human Needs,"

Development Paper No. 25 (Washington, D.C.: Overseas Development Council, 1978). For an earlier version cf. Hollis Chenery *et al.*, *Redistribution with Growth* (London: Oxford University Press, 1974).

19. Streeten is presently a Special Advisor to the Policy Planning and Program Review Department at the World Bank. See the following unpublished papers: "Basic Needs: An Issues Paper," Policy Planning and Program Review Department, World Bank, March 21, 1977, 21 pp.; and Streeten, "The Distinctive Features of a Basic Needs Approach to Development," August 1, 1977, 16 pp. Cf. Streeten, "Changing Perceptions of Development," *Finance and Development*, Vol. 14 No. 3 (September 1977), pp. 14–16, 40; also Streeten, "The Distinctive Features of a Basic Needs Approach to Development," *International Development Review*, Vol. XIX No. 3 (1977/3), pp. 8–16.

20. One approach to measurement is described in Morris David Morris and Florizelle B. Liser, "The POLI: Measuring Progress in Meeting Human Needs," *Communique on Development Issues*, No. 32, Washington, D.C.: Overseas Development Council, n.d.

21. Robert Packenham, *Liberal America and the Third World* (Princeton, N.J.: Princeton University Press, 1973).

22. I have discussed this problem at greater length in Denis Goulet, *Looking at Guinea-Bissau: A New Nation's Development Strategy*, Occasional Paper No. 9, Washington, D.C.: Overseas Development Council, 1977.

23. Many such efforts are described in Inter-American Foundation, *They Know How, An Experiment in Development Assistance* (Washington, D.C.: U.S. Government Printing Office, 1977).

24. On this see Denis Goulet, "World Hunger: Putting Development Ethics to the Test," *Sociological Enquiry*, Vol. 45 No. 4 (1975), pp. 3–9.

25. Gunnar Myrdal, *The Challenge of World Poverty* (New York: Pantheon, 1970), p. 277. Italics are Myrdal's.

26. For a sharply polemical statement of the contrasting positions see Edgar Z. Friedenberg, *The Disposal of Liberty and Other Industrial Wastes* (New York: Doubleday & Co., 1975).

27. On this see Denis Goulet, "Development and the International Economic Order," *International Development Review*, Vol. XVI No. 2 (1974), pp. 10–16. For a more exhaustive treatment, cf. Goulet, "Technology Transfers in Context: An Evolving World Order," in *The Uncertain Promise* (New York: IDOC Books, 1977), pp. 195–232.

28. This problem is discussed in Goulet, *The Cruel Choice*, *op. cit.*, pp. 241–249.

29. Arthur M. Okun, *Equality and Efficiency, The Big Tradeoff* (Washington, D.C.: The Brookings Institution, 1975).

30. Frances Moore Lappé and Joseph Collins, *Food First, Beyond the Myth of Scarcity* (Boston: Houghton Mifflin Co., 1977).

31. Erich Fromm, "Introduction," to *Socialist Humanism*, edited by Fromm (New York: Anchor Books, 1966), p. ix.

32. André van Dam, "Education About Global Development," *UNESCO/Mind Colloquium* (New London, Conn.: June 1974), p. 3.

33. Denis Goulet, "World Interdependence: Verbal Smokescreen or New Ethic?" *Development Paper*, No. 21 (Washington, D.C.: Overseas Development Council, March 1976), pp. 19–20.

34. Studies on "new approaches to aid" proliferate. For one example, see Lester E. Gordon *et al.*, Interim Report: *An Assessment of Development Assistance Strategies* (Washington, D.C.: The Brookings Institution, October 6, 1977). Cf. also Denis Goulet, "Notes on the Ethics of Development Assistance" in Krishna Kumar, ed., *Bonds Without Bondage: Explorations in Transnational Cultural Cooperation* (Honolulu: East-West Center Press, forthcoming). For a recent study of new approaches to "aid" by non-governmental organizations, see John G. Sommer, *Beyond Charity: U.S. Voluntary Aid for a Changing Third World* (Washington, D.C.: Overseas Development Council, 1977).

35. For one example see Marc Nerfin, ed., *Another Development: Approaches and Strategies* (Uppsala, Sweden: The Dag Hammarskjöld Foundation, 1977).

36. The notion of "vital nexus" is explained in Goulet, *The Uncertain Promise*, pp. 42–46.

Discussion Questions

1. Why do the critics and defenders of the traditional development strategy reach such contradictory conclusions concerning its success?

2. Does the U.S. have a real interest in helping the governments of the least developed countries meet the basic needs of the people there?

3. Is it inevitable that the poor textile or shoe workers in the U.S. must give up their jobs so that the poor in the least developed countries can have jobs exporting textiles and shoes?

4. The poor get what they grab. The only way the poor will get more is through their own power to force the developed countries to restructure the international economy, e.g., OPEC. Discuss.

5. We have a moral responsibility to help the governments of the least developed countries feed the hungry, clothe the naked, heal the sick. Discuss.

6. Discuss the importance of values in a basic human needs strategy of development. What is the relation between values and needs?

7. Goulet claims the central questions are: By whom are needs decided, and in response to which incentives? Discuss.

III
Agricultural Development
Perspective

U.S. Foreign Agricultural Development Policies: The Forces That Influence Change

Lyle P. Schertz

The United States has a preeminent position in the world in many activities. One of these important activities—international economic assistance—has been beset with continued criticism. And, in recent years Congress has directed that U.S. economic assistance give priority to programs that benefit poor people in poor countries, with emphasis in these efforts on food and agriculture.

Congressional directives and other major forces could lead to even further changes in U.S. policies affecting agriculture of the lower income countries. The likelihood for possible changes, however, can best be assessed by first having a perspective of the broad changes in policy which have occurred over the years and then reviewing some of the major and pervasive forces that have impinged upon these policy changes and are likely to have significant continuing influence.

I
DRAMATIC CHANGES IN U.S. POLICIES

A convenient approach is to consider the past thirty years. In terms of U.S. policy toward the agriculture of lower income countries, we can identify three periods characterized this way: A Period of Benign Neglect, 1947–1953; A Period of Inconsistency,

1953–1964; and A Period of Ambivalence but Improved Understanding, 1965–Present.

A Period of Benign Neglect, 1947–1953

In many ways U.S. international policies following post-World War II reflected pre-war attitudes and perceptions. Commercial considerations were prominent. The world was viewed as being composed of markets for U.S. exports, competitive exporters, and suppliers to the United States of needed imports.

In turn, restoration of productivity, income and trade in Europe and Japan was given high priority. This focus on the reconstruction of our adversaries included food and agriculture. It emphasized industrialization but also encompassed food and agriculture. The United States' unprecedented resource transfers to Europe under the Marshall Plan included large amounts of food, as well as developmental inputs such as hybrid corn, chemical fertilizers, and single purpose cattle bred for high yields of milk or beef. In Japan, land reform and food production were stressed in order to keep redundant labor employed in rural areas, to reduce dependency on U.S. food aid, and to destroy the power base of the Japanese ruling class.

A program to aid low-income countries that paralleled the Marshall Plan was Point IV. It focused on health, education, and agriculture, but the resources were meager and spread thinly compared to the resources provided to Europe and Japan. The United States avoided assistance for production of crops it exported.

A Period of Inconsistency, 1953–1964

The plight of the lower income countries (LIC) became recognized by the United States as a major world problem during the 1950s. Introduction of health measures drastically reduced developing world death rates, and economic demands accelerated, but growth in agricultural production lagged behind. Food imports by these countries expanded, but large numbers of people remained hungry.

Other major developments emerged and prompted policies inconsistent with the needs of low-income countries. The Cold War caused Europeans to worry about their food supplies and influenced the European community's protectionist Common Agricultural Policy. The British, experiencing balance-of-payments and budget problems, abandoned low-food price policies. In spite of expanding export markets, U.S. surpluses accumulated as U.S. agricultural productivity exploded. The increase of protectionism in agricultural trade and rising U.S. surpluses heavily influenced U.S. policies toward agricultural development in low-income countries. For example, the U.S. was interested in improved conditions in the poor countries. But, it was reluctant to aid the development of their agriculture for fear that expansion of food production in the poor countries would directly or indirectly substitute for U.S. exports.

The Western model of development—industrialize, create employment, facilitate migration of people from agriculture, and thereby set the stage for the restructuring of agriculture in ways that make it more efficient and productive—was emphasized in U.S. assistance programs.

Food aid was available to offset shortages of food supplies in these countries. This availability of food on concessional terms reflected the desire of the United States to expand agricultural exports even if substantial price discounts were required.

But this availability also reinforced the promotion of the Western model of development. Stable and low food prices were important adjuncts to industrialization and expansion of urban employment in the poor countries. And food aid in many cases was an essential means of supplementing domestic supplies. It saved scarce foreign exchange for purchases of imports required for industrialization.

The principal decisionmakers in the LIC also liked this approach. In these countries, the finance ministers typically had the major role in deciding on international assistance and development strategies. They had little empathy for rural people. The availability of food aid permitted them to pursue industrialization and to ignore needed investments and farm prices necessary for accelerating food production increases.

While food and agriculture ministers had relatively greater interest in investments and prices favorable to agriculture, their political influence on development strategies was typically weak, and in many cases they were not even consulted on P.L. 480 agreements. (Public Law 480 enabled LICs to pay for agricultural products in their own currencies. The U.S. agreed not to convert these currencies into dollars. This saved the LICs from having to spend scarce foreign exchange.) Thus, while many country officials professed interest in the food and agriculture they were often ambivalent as to the priority they placed on improved production by farmers and greater food consumption by the hungry.

The Western model of development and associated policies were also embraced by U.S. leaders. USDA leadership was not interested in promoting LIC agricultural development. While USDA had had significant responsibilities for foreign development work in the late 1940s and early 1950s, Secretary Benson wanted to be rid of it. He participated actively in developing plans for the transfer of all USDA foreign agricultural development programs and related personnel to the AID predecessor agency. This transfer set the stage for the present day situation in which AID presently has only a woefully limited number of people on its staff with technical training in nutrition, food, or agriculture and only a few, if any, at top-level decision-making positions.

The emphasis on the Western development model, supported with concessional food aid, helped with the directors of U.S. economic assistance programs. Congressional actions led to cumbersome and often difficult review and budget procedures for activities financed with appropriations to AID. In contrast, food aid had not been encumbered to the same extent, thus facilitating more independent actions by directors of U.S. economic assistance on the use of the resources associated with P.L. 480 agreements.

This independence was also facilitated by USDA emphasis on market development and its limited interest in agricultural development of the recipient countries. USDA had only limited interest in how the local currencies generated by sales of P.L. 480 commodities were utilized.

But, alas, we see now that given (1) the extent to which the industrial world was willing to open its markets to imports from the LICs and (2) the amount of economic assistance that was to be made available for the development of these poor countries, the Western model was not consistent with the needs of the developing countries.

Industrialization was hampered by the lack of administrative and technical skills in these countries. Transportation and communications were woefully lacking and they remained deficient even though economic aid made large contributions to their improvements. Labor intensive technology was not available. Western technology was transferred, but it was not optimum because it was capital intensive. Over time, these limitations may have been overcome if LIC export demand had not been hampered by trade restraints or if economic assistance had been substantially larger.

A Period of Ambivalence
but Improved Understanding, 1965–Present

In the past decade or so, Americans have developed a better understanding of food and hunger problems in low-income countries. In turn, Americans, although divided in their opinions, may be increasingly prepared to support steps which lead to the realization by hungry people of their "right to food." Reflecting this increasing support but divided opinion by Americans there remains substantial ambivalence among U.S. political institutions as to how the United States should organize to relate to this new setting.

The mid-1960s marked the start of a dramatic shift in U.S. policy that was expressed in legislation. One set of developments was triggered by the magnitude of the India food problems in the mid-1960s. India's heavy reliance on food aid forced a reconsideration of development strategies. The serious production shortages in 1964 and 1966 led to heavy reliance on P.L. 480. These developments also afforded an opportunity for those critical of past development strategies to press for dramatic changes in the U.S. approach to LIC development.

In turn, P.L. 480 legislation was amended extensively. "Self-help" provisions called for explicit considerations of LIC agricultural strategies and required the termination of agreements if LIC governments failed to comply with self-help provisions included in the agreements. Tropical and subtropical agricultural research, as well as farmer to farmer programs, were to be activities administered by the USDA.

These amendments signaled dissatisfaction by the Congress with the way in which the Executive Branch had neglected agricultural development in the LICs and had neglected research focused on food problems of the LICs. These changes proved also to be forerunners of other more recent changes in U.S. economic assistance legislation that has emphasized the need to concentrate U.S. efforts on food and other basic needs and implementing programs so that they help the poor.

Changes over time in international food needs and international market prices have led to a somewhat better understanding by Americans of the nature of hunger in the world. There is a better realization that the food needs of the LICs could be too large for the United States to supply them. Consequently, emphasis must be placed on improving food production and employment within these countries if hunger is to be reduced substantially.

But U.S. policies and organizations are not easily changed—one factor was sheer momentum. In other cases, response to the newly perceived needs would have meant conflict with U.S. domestic objectives and/or aggravation of U.S. domestic problems.

The self-help provisions of P.L. 480 provide an example of the problems that a change in policy can encounter. Effective implementation of self help of P.L. 480 would have required some combination of:

- Greater involvement with P.L. 480 agreements of LIC ministries of food and agriculture as well as ministries of finance.
- Greater involvement of U.S. food and agricultural development experts in negotiation of P.L. 480 agreements—a domain largely,

though not exclusively, claimed by program officers and embassy officials with backgrounds in trade, finance, and industrial development, but not food and agricultural development.

- A greater responsibility for USDA to oversee how recipient countries utilized P.L. 480 generated resources in support of food and agricultural development objectives.
- Within USDA, resource availabilities to support staff activities focused on food and agricultural development as well as trade, in consideration of P.L. 480 programs.
- Changes in the Executive Order signed by President Eisenhower which delineated responsibilities within the Executive Branch for the implementation of P.L. 480.

But changes that involve departures from traditional approaches and in some cases shifts in participation in decision making are slow in coming.

The ambivalence regarding the mix of USDA-AID inputs to the administration of P.L. 480 is somewhat reflected in levels of USDA international assistance over time. As mentioned earlier, Secretary Benson preferred to avoid involvement of USDA in foreign development work. In contrast, Secretary Freeman pressed for a larger voice by the department in country program development. In fact, at the time of the Indian crisis he was ordered by President Johnson to become intimately involved. However, it was not until the last budget prepared by President Johnson that appropriations were proposed for USDA to carry out tropical and subtropical research as authorized in the 1966 changes in P.L. 480.

Secretary Butz did not encourage the involvement of USDA in P.L. 480 self help. In 1976 Congressman Findley pressed for USDA tò embrace what last year became Title XII of the foreign assistance act, which calls for a much closer linkage of U.S. universities to foreign economic development and greater emphasis on research focused on the problems of the LICs. But, Secretary Butz refused that it be made part of the USDA responsibilities.

On the other hand, over the years many USDA experts have helped staff the AID technical cooperation programs and training activities.

Congressional activities reflect ambivalence also:

- Congress passed the amendments to P.L. 480 in 1966, but did not insist on their implementation.
- It more recently passed the 75% rule which requires that 75% of Title I food aid must go to countries most seriously affected by food shortages and lack of foreign exchange.
- It also instructed the Executive to aggressively pursue arrangements with recipient countries whereby debt associated with P.L. 480 is forgiven when countries agree to use associated resources for important food and agricultural development activities.
- It also amended foreign assistance legislation, calling for new directions, with the intention that U.S. economic assistance would benefit the poorest people in developing countries and principally through aid to agriculture and rural development.
- It passed the Title XII amendments which call for a much closer linkage of U.S. universities to foreign economic development and greater emphasis on research focused on the problems of the lower income countries.
- It passed the 1977 Farm Act which included a section directing the USDA to become a more active participant in international research.
- It displayed considerable anxiety at the same time about world developments such as increased palm oil production and trade. And loans by international financial institutions have been criticized by Congressional interests.

To a significant extent actions by Congress reflect the shifting opinions of the various groups in our society. For example, over the past 30 years the private voluntary organizations have made substantial contributions to development overseas. And in addition their educational efforts among the American public have been a major force leading to a better understanding of world food problems and, in turn, an increased political support for U.S. international assistance.

In spite of the ambivalence about how the United Nations should organize to relate to the new setting, the 1965 to present period taken as a whole has been one in which Americans have come to realize more fully the dimensions of the food problems of low income countries. And with this greater understanding, there appears to be a greater willingness by Americans to support programs that focus on hunger. At the same time substantial suspicions continue about possible linkages between U.S. economic assistance and U.S. military and political objectives. And, many question if the U.S. Government has the management capacity to operate effectively a foreign assistance program focused on poor people and on nutrition, food, and agriculture.

II
FORCES STIMULATING POLICY CHANGES

The first section of this article identified several factors which affected U.S. policies toward agricultural development in the developing countries. Some of the more prominent were:

• The successful support to European and Japanese recovery.
• The role of industrialization in the West and the inclination to transplant this approach to the poor countries.
• The large productive capacity of U.S. agriculture.
• The Indian food problems of the mid-1960s.
• The growing import requirements of the developing countries.

But there have been other major and pervasive forces that have had a major influence on the policy changes. Further, these other forces help explain why Americans understand world food problems better today than they did 10 to 20 years ago and why there appears to be a genuine concern by an increasing number of Americans for the hungry of other countries.

Four of these factors are closely related:

• New discontinuities in relations among nations.
• Obvious effects of wealth and income on food distribution.
• Greater interdependence among countries of the world.
• Nuclear proliferation.

New Discontinuities in Relations among Nations

The 1970s have witnessed great discontinuities in relations among nations. Decisions of the Organization of Petroleum Exporting Countries (OPEC) have caused sharp changes in the distribution of incomes and in turn the wealth among nations. Detente with the USSR and the People's Republic of China led to increased East-West trade and reduced cold war motivations in foreign aid programs.

Political organizations of LICs, such as the formation of the group of 77 of the low income countries, in pressing their demands on the developed countries have forced the United States and other developed countries to consider more seriously the effects of trade policies and international assistance not only on Americans and Europeans but on the lower income countries. These intensified pressures by LICs for better terms of trade and distribution of goods, including food, are likely to continue.

Effects of Wealth and Income on Food Distribution

Today, people in developing nations, which includes two-thirds of the world's population, eat only one-fourth of the world's protein, mostly in the form of cereals. In countries such as India, people consume less than 400 pounds of cereals per capita each year. On the other hand, in developed countries, large quantities of cereals are converted to protein. Annual per capita grain equivalent consumption is 1,435 pounds in the USSR, about 1,800 pounds in the Federal Republic of Germany and France, and 1,850 pounds in the United States. The billion people in the rich nations, with tastes for livestock products, use practically as much cereal for livestock feed as the two billion people in the LICs use directly as food.

While population growth has obviously been a significant factor in increasing world food demand, even more striking has been the sharp recent increase in cereal consumption per capita in developed countries where populations have not been growing rapidly. In the 8-year period, 1964–66 to 1972–74, per capita consumption of cereal grains increased by 250 pounds, or 16 percent, in the United States and by 330 pounds, or 30 percent, in the USSR. These gains were more than half the 1972–74 total consumption of 395 pounds per capita in developing countries.

The USSR's decision to protect upgraded diets was felt worldwide by both rich and poor. When the Soviets purchased almost one-fifth of the total U.S. wheat supply in the 1972–73 crop year, supplies normally available to others dropped sharply. Nations and people reacted by bidding up the price of the remaining wheat, the more aggressively because currencies of Japan and several other commercial importers of U.S. foodstuffs were worth substantially more in terms of dollars as a result of successive devaluations.

In contrast, the limited wealth and low income of poor countries again determined how well they could compete in food purchasing. So long as total cereal production is adequate for needs, effects on the poor are minimal, especially over time. But in times of sharply increased demand or curtailed supplies, impacts can be harsh. For example, the 1972–73 Indian food grain crop dropped from 105 million to 96 million tons. In the tug-of-war between maintaining diets and saving foreign exchange, diets lost and food prices were allowed to increase. In some areas, food grain rations were cut in half in fair-price food shops, which serve many of the lowest income Indians. Per capita calorie availability dropped toward the critical levels of the mid-1960s. (In considering effects of wealth and income on distribution of food, it is important to distinguish between short run and long run. In the short run, the world is dealing with food already produced or about to be produced. Distribution of income among rich and poor is then a primary determinant of the distribution of food. In contrast, response of producers over time is an important consideration in the long-run. For example, production in the past has been responsive to demand flowing from incomes. Thus, in the long-run, low incomes of low-income nations have been a primary determinant of low food consumption levels of these countries, but high incomes of developed countries have not.)

The resulting wide fluctuations in prices, the associated impacts of high prices on low income countries, and the seeming permanency of hunger in low income countries despite low U.S. farm prices has led an increasing number of Americans to question whether wealth and income should continue to have an overwhelming effect on distribution of food and, therefore, on the incidence of hunger in the world.

Greater Interdependence among Countries of the World

Both of the first two forces discussed in this section have reinforced the concept that the world is interdependent. The food price problems of 1972–77 provided first hand lessons for each of us. The energy problems have reinforced this perception and brought us all to realize increasingly that developments in other countries can have substantial impacts on our welfare. The interrelationships among people of the world has been illustrated also by the successful development of new cereal technologies at the international research centers in Mexico and in the Philippines and the introduction of these technologies in many countries. There, scientists literally remade wheat, rice, and maize plants. Many of the scientists had been trained in the United States, many had previously worked with the USDA and in U.S. universities. And U.S. science and technology was an important part of the knowledge upon which these efforts were based. The payoffs to the lower income countries have been substantial. In 1975 for example, over 100 million acres of wheat and rice were planted to the high yielding varieties in developing countries of Asia and the Near East, with significant impacts on food supplies. It works both ways too. Russian scientists pioneered in soil science before 1900 and we built on their work. Russian wheats made important contributions to U.S. wheat breeding programs. Americans cooperating with Africans have more recently developed techniques for maize breeding which have been highly useful in the U.S.

Through modern communications, these and other forces are leading millions of Americans to increasingly realize that the incomes of American farmers, the budgets of American consumers, subsidies for U.S. maritime interests are closely related to food policy decisions in the Kremlin, poverty in Northeast Brazil, drought in the Sahel, and empty food bowls in Bangladesh.

Nuclear Proliferation

An increasing number of nations have nuclear capability. In turn, the chances have increased markedly for individuals or groups of individuals to come into possession of weapons which can be used for international blackmail. These increased chances have come about in a world where those who are hungry and deprived of material goods know, through modern communications, that others are not deprived. This awareness could lead the people of these countries at least to tolerate if not support the use of nuclear blackmail to force redistribution of incomes and wealth among nations.

To sum up, U.S. foreign agricultural development policies have changed dramatically. After World War II the lower income countries were first neglected. Then policies inconsistent with the needs of low-income countries were pursued. The Western model of industrialization was prescribed but did not meet the serious problems of large scale underemployment and unemployment and associated limited economic demands. Americans more recently have developed a much better understanding of food and hunger problems in low-income countries. Although divided in their opinions they are increasingly prepared to support efforts that effectively relieve hunger among the poor. But substantial uncertainties about U.S. assistance continue to prevail.

New discontinuities in relations among nations such as the continuing role of OPEC, the close association of poverty and hunger, the direct and indirect effects of actions by one country on life and death of people in other countries, and the increasing number of countries with nuclear capabilities have been important factors undergirding these changes in attitudes of the American public.

Implications of Integrated Rural Development

Albert Waterston

With marvelous perspicuity, Paul Streeten once remarked that economists, who should know better, tend to give way to fashion or ideology to explain complex economic events with a single factor. He pointed out that this tendency goes back a long way. The Physiocrats stressed land as the source of all wealth (as development was called in those olden days); and while mercantilists thought it was gold, classical economists insisted it was labor. More recently, especially with the ascendancy of econometric development models, many economists have asserted that capital was the strategic variable in development.

In recent years, as development has moved toward the center of the economic stage, this penchant for over-simplification has been noteworthy in the field of development, the road to which—despite its manifest rockiness and complexity—repeatedly has been explained or defined with beguiling simplicity. Moreover, in keeping with the speedup of everything in the current era, it is explained every few years in a different way, as one fad succeeds another.

Thus, development was conceived, not very long ago, as being the same as growth of per capita income; then, as this now obvious absurdity was exposed, as growth plus change; next, it was seen as the mitigation if not the abolition of poverty, unemployment and economic discrimination; then, with soaring optimism, as liberation; only to collapse pessimistically to the nadir of zero growth. But not for long: The optimists among the practitioners of the dismal science soon seized the initiative with theories of rural, then urban development, to be followed by a theory of growth-cum-equitable distribution; only to be challenged lately by a theory that conceives development as the meeting of basic needs of people. And before this one can be digested one hears of yet another theory—(or is it a sub-theory?)—about to burst forth from the wings which holds that a basic needs strategy must include a theory of human rights.

As the theories have appeared, thicker and faster with the passage of time, each jostling the others for the spotlight, one has had the feeling that there is something right with each. How many development economists do not from time to time still refer to the per capita income of a country as a measure of its development? And if there was an outcry from the development fraternity when Simon Kuznets, the man who made us aware of the fact that growth and change were inseparable in the development process, received a Nobel Memorial Prize for his work, it was not discernible. Who would deny that development is a misnomer when accompanied by increased poverty, unemployment and economic discrimination? And as Arthur Lewis said years ago, a country's development can be measured by the extent to which it can exercise control over its economy, so who would not accept liberation from outside intervention as an indicator of development? In a materialistic world bent on lopsided consumption of scarce resources, no-growth can appear to be the only way to stop the crazy careening down the social mountainside to world self-destruction; and only the most heartless can oppose improvement of the lot of the poor through integrated rural development or urban renewal theories, augmented by thoughtful economists who demonstrate—despite the dismal historical record—that growth, and equitable distribution of the fruits thereof, can be bedfellows. And the basic needs approach to development, cannot this be viewed—as Paul Streeten has suggested—as "the culmination of 25 years of development thought and experience"? For, as he says, the basic needs approach can be thought of as embracing components of earlier "strategies and approaches, such as rural development, urban poverty alleviation, . . . 'redistribution with growth,' and other poverty-employment-and-equity-oriented approaches."

The search for an all-encompassing theory of development drives economists on from partial to holistic theories. Thus it was that "selective" rural development—which has been defined as covering one or more non-agricultural rural activities, like transport or improvement of health or education—gave way to "integrated" rural development defined as inter-related multi-sectoral rural development activities which include agriculture; and thus it is that "integrated" rural development now appears on the verge of being over-shadowed by the basic needs approach.

Not that the concept of integrated rural development can be considered unduly narrow. For while a generally acceptable definition of integrated rural development has not been devised, integrated rural development as usually conceived, not only includes agriculture, agro-industry, social infrastructure, and welfare services or programs, but also aims at raising the general level of well-being of rural peoples (in contrast to the objective of agricultural development which more narrowly aims, usually, at merely increasing the level of agricultural output and its distribution).

Yet, given the administrative and political constraints in developing countries, it is dubious whether the concept of "integrated" rural development can withstand a hard look. The idea of organically-interrelated rural development is so appealing it might appear that only the most bilious person would quarrel with it. Nevertheless, arguments which have been mustered against the now almost forgotten balanced development approach appear to be equally valid against the integrated rural development approach. Not only are the administrative constraints in developing countries so formidable that they would make a travesty of attempts to develop their rural sector by holistic approaches such as are implied by the integrated rural development approach; it is unlikely that most developing countries are sufficiently committed to the concept to allocate the necessary resources.

For the fact is that the concept of integrated rural development is an export from developed parts of the world (which of course includes the World Bank), fabricated from successes in partial approaches to rural development in a few countries like Taiwan, Malaysia, and Israel. And since the concept of "integrated" rural development was conceived far from the scene of these successes, largely by persons whose experience did not include field activities in the countries where these successes (and failures) occurred, it is not surprising that the approach to integrated rural development is flawed by a series of misapprehensions about the problems associated with the implementation of rural development projects and programs.

As already indicated, one of these misapprehensions has to do with the holistic approach to these problems. An organically-interrelated program of rural development requires a degree of coordination of policies, inputs, administrative procedures and organizational structures which does not exist even in most developed countries, let alone developing countries. Before an integrated program of rural development could be carried out in most agricultural countries, major re-orientations in pricing, marketing and resource allocation policies would have to occur; methods of handling seeds, tools, fertilizers and water supplies would have to be modernized; constraints imposed by lethargic, if not actively hostile, bureaucracies would have to be substantially mitigated; organizations working in rural development would have to learn the benefits of mutual cooperation instead of confrontation and competition; and cultural and traditional modes of behavior inherent in most peasant societies would have to be dealt with in appropriate ways. These things can be achieved, but only by programs of training people in improved management at different levels, programs which are lacking in most "integrated" rural development projects. The need for training people engaged in rural development activities is barely understood by most sponsors of integrated rural development; or if understood, largely ignored because of the excessive hurry to show statistical results for large financial investments in such projects and programs.

The size of these investments constitutes a second misapprehension about how to go about implementing rural development projects and programs: Those who favor an integrated approach to rural development believe that most problems associated with this approach can be overcome with more money, supervised of course by a central sponsoring body or agency. For example, the World Bank is fond of announcing how much its loans for rural development have increased.[1] There is undoubtedly a need for more capital in rural communities throughout the world, but it should be obvious that much more than money is needed to achieve integrated rural development—or any other kind; and that supervision of the way money is spent by a central agency or body is not enough to insure effective rural development.

This is the lesson of history.[2] A large and well-publicized rural development program is Mexico's PIDER program, which is estimated to cost $1.2 billion, of which World Bank loans account for $230 million. But in spite of the efforts of the Mexican Government, as well as the World Bank and the Inter-American Development Bank, reliable estimates place the proportion of farmers in the target group who have been helped by the program at no more than about 20% of the total. Loans to help Indonesia's poor farmers have had even poorer results.

That much more than money is required to help the poor, whether urban or rural, in developed countries as well as undeveloped ones, was revealed by a recent United Press International (UPI) investigation of the anti-poverty effort launched by President Lyndon B. Johnson in 1964 as the center piece of his Great Society program. Since 1964, the U.S. has spent more than $22 billion in the name of the poor, enough—some say—to lift every man, woman and child in the U.S. out of poverty three times over. Yet, an estimated 26 million Americans remain beneath the $5,850 poverty line for a family of four.

Every rural development project which falls short of achieving its target furnishes its own set of reasons for partial or substantial failure. As already indicated, shortcomings of policy, administrative and organizational constraints, and sociological or political factors often play important roles. Money spent on even what appear to be worthwhile projects oriented toward helping poor farmers may end up helping the rich, the middle class, or some other unintended groups. Sometimes, governments are unable to prepare and carry out rural development programs at a desirable rate. This can leave large sums unspent, as the World Bank discovered in Indonesia. *The Wall Street Journal*, in its issue of November 10, 1977, pointed out that Indonesia's inability to put available funds to good use had forced the World Bank to rein in its plans to lend more money to Indonesia. The Government was simply unable to prepare and carry out programs at the desired rate. And the Government was as lacking as the Bank in people and knowledge to deal effectively with large numbers of small loans.

The inability to absorb money fast enough can also lead to the diversion of funds to activities ostensibly helpful to the poor but actually of little value to them. The UPI investigation of President Johnson's anti-poverty program, previously referred to, found that millions of dollars were spent on studies, surveys, research reports and data retrieval systems, much of which ended up unused on government shelves. The chief beneficiaries appear to have been economists, other academic researchers, consultants and "experts."

It is not news to say that a similar situation prevails in developing countries. As Richard Critchfield put it in *RF Illustrated*,[3] the publication of the Rockefeller Foundation, assistance to poor countries "tends to become so enveloped in rhetoric, paper work, conferences, jet flights, and the maintenance of the development professional's own living standards that the ultimate connection with helping poor people can get lost."

In a Congressional investigation of the Johnson anti-poverty program, the House Government Operations Committee found that the program produced inexperienced or self-seeking groups which led to instances of mismanagement and outright corruption, and produced "major areas of weakness, inefficiency and graft." In Indonesia, in connection with a World Bank loan to rebuild the country's sugar industry, inadequate payments to farmers from the sugar companies were intercepted by corrupt officials who forced the unhappy farmers to grow sugarcane at gunpoint. Similar examples can be given in other countries.

A third misapprehension, related to the "big money" approach, may be called the "big project" approach. Donor countries or international agencies are necessarily compelled to show that they are cost-effective. This is hard to do for small rural development projects. Thus, Montague Yudelman's paper, previously referred to, makes the point that "lending to large-scale producers is in general less costly than lending to small-scale producers; administrative costs of loans to large producers are often in the neighborhood of 3 or 4 percent of outstanding loans; administrative costs of loans . . . to small producers tend to range from 10 to 20 percent. These costs do not include any charge for the use of capital, so an interest rate for small farmers that would cover both capital and administrative costs could be as high as 30 percent." Preoccupation with financial efficiency in the short-term, rather than with a longer-term social objective of spreading the fruits of well-being as widely as possible, as well as the need to supervise loans with small staffs, leads to a bias in favor of large loans. It usually takes as much time and staff to extend and to supervise effectively a small loan as a large one. Moreover, lending agencies have built up expertise in dealing with large loans which often cannot be applied as easily to small loans.

But experience shows that rural development requires mostly large numbers of small loans involving local activities. Most of those concerned with rural development would accept this as fact, especially with regard to the implementation of rural development projects; some would also accept this as fact with regard to the formulation of rural development projects and programs; but very few of those concerned with rural development understand the implications of this or, if they understand them, are in practice willing to yield the authority required to farmers.

This leads to a fourth misapprehension about rural development, which may be called the "centralization-versus-decentralization" argument. The *Wall Street Journal* story previously referred to described how much trickier it was to improve the life of the rural poor in Indonesia than it was to build roads, dams or other infrastructure projects in that country. The article cited specific instances which demonstrated that when the central government got down to the local level, it quickly was engulfed in cultural and political crosscurrents with which it could not cope. Jakarta, the capital, was too far from the villages to deal effectively with local needs and problems. The article concluded that the Government did not have the people required to "comprehend the chemistry of large numbers of small villages."

There are still many officials and others concerned with rural development who believe that rural development can be controlled from the capital of a country or even from a foreign or international base. These people spend much time deploring farmers' unwillingness to participate in carrying out national plans for rural development. But even if it is assumed that these individuals constitute a minority, those who are relatively more enlightened—who believe that rural development requires decentralization to local or regional levels—do not usually go far enough, either in practice or in their thinking. In practice, many of these persons believe that farmers "participate" in the preparation of a rural development project, program or plan if their opinions are sought out by officials about what needs to be done. Even in this limited sense, participation has sometimes turned out to be a charade in practice, when farmers' opinions have been ignored during the formulation of rural development projects, programs and plans. In what one hopes was an extreme case—it happened in Mexico in connection with the PIDER project—farmers in one area who had requested a milk plant when canvassed by central planners, were given a latrine![4]

In their thinking, most authorities involved in rural development projects and programs do not understand that farmers are usually much more informed than are the authorities about the production possibilities of the land the farmers work and about what farmers' objectives should be. What the authorities often fail to grasp is that what the farmer lacks are the techniques to achieve his own objectives. Because of this it is the authorities who must "participate" in achieving farmers' objectives, not the other way around.

Governmental authorities must realize that their own points of view and those of farmers usually differ greatly. The way they look at farmers may not be in the best interest of farmers, and farmers may know this. Where farmers' objectives do not coincide with national objectives, authorities need to find ways of harmonizing the two, but always with due regard to farmers' objectives. This is essential because when farmers are asked by the authorities to alter their objectives, it is the farmers who run the greater risk in case of failure. The authorities must remember that farmers always have the veto power if authorities try to force them into activities with which the farmers do not agree.

Related to the "centralization-decentralization" misapprehension—indeed, a part of the problem—is the widespread failure of officials and others concerned with rural development to understand that much more could be done by farmers themselves, in the form of increased investment of their surplus labor (a generally unused source of rural capital accumulation). At the peasant's level, the most abundant resource is usually labor. Experience demonstrates that when appropriately motivated poor farmers will increase the use of their labor on farm improvements. Experience in Taiwan, China and elsewhere also reveals that the best way to motivate farmers is "from the bottom up" by the use of self-help techniques, assisted from the "top down" as required. "Top-down" assistance should take the form of appropriate financial incentives (including rational price policies for agricultural commodities) and other inducements which encourage farmers to engage in self-help activities.

In some countries, governments need to disabuse farmers of the notion—frequently nurtured by governments themselves— that all development activities must be carried out by government; in other countries, governments only have to eliminate constraints which prevent self-help activities from emerging; in all countries, governments have to provide incentives and inducements to accelerate self-help and self-reliance.

To do these things requires major reshaping of the policies, as well as administrative procedures and organizational structures, in developing countries. Given the predilections of most of these governments, much time and effort are likely to be expended before appreciable changes are made. Meanwhile priority should be given to training poor people at the local level in rural communities to increase their ability to absorb funds becoming available to a greater extent than ever before for rural development (thanks to the emphasis now being given to rural development). This implies the training of poor people in rural areas in self-help techniques.

In this connection, surprisingly good results sometimes have been obtained by private, usually foreign, voluntary organizations, both religious and secular. In virtually every instance, these successes have been registered by individuals stationed at the local level for years at a time, living with the peasants in their villages or localities and working with them in a spirit of mutual respect and an understanding of what it means to eke out a living on a peasant farm. These activities need to be augmented with more money, but even more, with additional volunteers who are committed! Sometimes, private, voluntary organizations have helped carry out nutrition and other programs in cooperation with rural development projects financed by the World Bank. There is need for greatly expanding such cooperation. Even when private, voluntary organizations have had on-going relations with a national government (as is often essential), the actual work done was almost always carried out at the local level. Local activities are an essential ingredient in successful rural development.

The U.S. government-to-government counterpart to foreign, private, voluntary organizations—the Peace Corps—was and is the most successful U.S. effort ever carried out to help the poor in the poor countries. It is a pity that changing priorities in the United States have reduced the Peace Corps to almost a third the size it had in its heyday during the Kennedy Administration. This trend needs to be reversed and there is hope that it will be under the Carter Administration. There is a debate in progress about whether the Peace Corps needs more technicians or more generalists. One would think it obvious that both are needed, provided they are dedicated to work with the poor where they live and work. Anyone with experience knows that intelligent generalists can be taught enough about a subject in a short time to do surprisingly good work, especially if they are supervised by a qualified technician to whom they can turn for help when needed. What an opportunity exists today for the United States to make use of now unused human resources in this country for the benefit of poverty-stricken mankind in poor countries—and in this country as well!

The work of a compassionate person working directly with poor people can make a tremendous difference to the poor. A Jesuit priest trained in modern fishing techniques has greatly raised the level of living of fishermen with whom he lived for 10 years in the fishing village of Itapua, in the Brazilian state of Bahia. An energetic economics professor has helped a hundred or so small slum enterprises get management advice and loans in Bahia and raised the level of living of the people with whom he worked. Many young people just out of graduate school have found rewarding work in rural communities working in nutrition and related fields.

Taken by themselves these projects are drops in the bucket

compared with what needs to be done. The problem with "small is beautiful" is that while small may be beautiful, by definition it remains small. What is needed is a way of establishing means for replicating these small activities in a perpetuating and expanding system, while improving performance in a systematic way.

Here is a field where universities could play a significant role. By combining research to this end, with teaching and field work of the kind described, universities could seek to uncover principles for expanding, perpetuating and improving people-to-people development activities from the bottom up. From among their student bodies they could enlist those who wish to participate in this worthwhile and rewarding endeavor. Experience shows that there are many who would be eager to enroll, given the opportunity. Some of my own ex-students have enrolled with private, voluntary organizations and spent several years working at local levels in Kenya, the Sudan, Guatemala, Thailand, Jordan and elsewhere. Virtually without exception, they report great personal satisfaction with their experience. Frequently, they seek additional experience in the same or different countries because the satisfaction obtained in working with the poor in rural communities exceeds anything they can find in other fields.

I hope—and have proposed—that the American University, with which I am associated, will establish a Development Center which combines scholarship and experience in this triad of field work, research and teaching to come to grips with the complexities and hardships involved in helping the desperately poor—whether they be located abroad or in the United States.

Such a Development Center could become a hub for a network of private, voluntary organizations engaged in helping the poor. These organizations often lack the fiscal and financial competence required to administer programs. A Development Center could train persons working in these fields in the theory and practice of management techniques including a systematic way of translating ideas into action. Students and faculty with field experience could carry out research and teach with the added authority gained from their experience; not only would this approach represent a departure from the often sterile "career education" characteristic of American universities, through the linking of education with relevant aspects of human life; it would enlist university talent to help lift the level of living of the poor.

American universities can learn much in this activity from the Chinese experience. While that experience may not be fully applicable in every instance, the desirability of educational policies which promote faculty and student participation in useful productive work in the fields with which they are associated is being increasingly recognized as a sound principle of education. In the light of what we have learned in recent years, the promise in this approach appears to be far greater than the "top down" and watered down "bottom up" approach now being followed to achieve rural development, whether "integrated" or "selective."

NOTES

1. Thus a paper by John Adler of the World Bank, entitled, "Development Aid for the Small Farmer—Expectations and Experience," boasted that between 1974 and 1977, the amount of Bank "lending for rural development increased from $450 million to $1,453 million." And another paper "The Role of Agriculture in Integrated Rural Development Projects—The Experience of the World Bank," by Montague Yudelman, says that since 1946 the World Bank has lent nearly $8 billion for agriculture and rural development. It also claims that "Inasmuch as each dollar invested by the Bank is generally matched by an equivalent investment from domestic resources the Bank has in the past 30 years contributed to and participated in the financing of some $16 billion in project-oriented programs in agriculture and rural development. . . . The contribution of the Bank has increased substantially in recent years, however, rising from an average of $120 million a year in the mid-1960s to more than $1.6 billion a year in the mid-1970s."

2. While the capital stock in agriculture has grown greatly in the last decade, agricultural output or the level of welfare of poor farmers has hardly increased.

3. Vol. 3, No. 4, September 1977.

4. It is all reminiscent of Theodore Levitt's account of a medieval priest's description of the social hierarchy in his time, a description which, with little change, applies in many countries today: "First, there's the King, then the nobility, then the gentry, then the merchants, tradesmen, the laborers, then there is nothing and again nothing, and once more nothing. Then there are the peasants. It's a long way to the top, especially if you don't know the way."

Discussion Questions

1. Will it be possible to decrease the number of hungry people in the world? Can hunger be eliminated?

2. Can hunger be significantly mitigated without changes in the distribution of income and wealth among nations and within countries?

3. Many U.S. farmers fear that reserves will dampen U.S. farm prices. Yet many people in the United States see that food reserves are essential if availability of food aid is to be assured and if wide gyrations in international prices are to be avoided. What is the appropriate way to strike a balance among these interrelated objectives?

4. Would a different "packaging" of U.S. assistance enhance the support of the U.S. public for these programs? Would it make a difference if programs directly related to food were organizationally separate from programs designed for general economic and security assistance?

5. Which changes in approach are needed to insure effective rural development projects and programs?

6. How can we mobilize the resources of our committed youth to meet the needs of the wretchedly poor of the world?

IV
Employment Perspective

Employment Problems in a Global Perspective

Paul G. Schervish

In our time the global economy has intensified its assault on the well-being and dignity of vast numbers of workers and their families.

Francis Blanchard, the Director-General of the International Labor Office (ILO) laments that a significant proportion of the world's population "continues to eke out an existence in the most abject conditions of material deprivation":

More than 700 million people live in acute poverty and are destitute. At least 460 million persons were estimated to suffer from a severe degree of protein-energy malnutrition even before the recent food crisis. Scores of millions live constantly under a threat of starvation. Countless millions suffer from debilitating diseases of various sorts and lack access to the most basic medical services. The squalor of urban slums is too well-known to need further emphasis. The number of illiterate adults has been estimated to have grown from 700 million in 1960 to 760 million towards 1970. The tragic waste of human resources in the Third World is symbolised by nearly 300 million persons unemployed or underemployed in the mid-1970s (1976: 3).

While statistics such as these never capture the full depth of human misery, they do summarize its extent and discomfort the complacent. Even so, it is not enough to describe the deprivation of unemployment, underemployment, economic insecurity, and toil of labor that haunt the lives of hundreds of millions of people.

97

In the end the goal must be to understand the causes of such plight and to transform the economic, political, and cultural forces that pass on from one generation to another an endless struggle for daily bread.

This article examines the global employment problem as it affects Third World market economies. It focuses on how this employment problem arises from the pattern of uneven and interdependent development of advanced and dependent societies and from the way this dependent development creates distorted employment structures within these Third World nations. The object is to explain the roots of the world employment problem by showing how the vast array of employment problems in the Third World are intricately woven threads in the fabric of domination that everywhere emerges from the global expansion of profit-motivated economic activity. In a word, employment problems affecting individual workers and their families in the Third World manifest the fundamental problem of how employment structures in the Third World are subject to and distorted by investment practices originating in board rooms located in the advanced market economies.

The first section of the article documents the unrelenting tyranny of employment problems and poverty plaguing the Third World. It summarizes the current plight and reports some projections for the future. The second section explains how such employment problems arise from the very nature and meaning of employment in market economies. It shows how the relentless search for profit by corporations in both the advanced industrial and underdeveloped nations distorts the economic growth of dependent nations and makes their employment structures incapable of adequately employing their populations.

The perspective of the article is sociological rather than economic. It emphasizes the social causes and consequences of employment and work in the Third World.

Much research on development concludes by recommending that jobs can be created and incomes raised by increasing investment in the Third World and by extending modern economic practices to outlying regions of the underdeveloped nations. While such proposals seem not only helpful but necessary, this article suggests a set of considerations that hopefully will make us pause and ask serious questions before lining up behind even the most thoughtful and sympathetic sounding proposals. These questions are not the questions of international lending institutions, of employers, or even of Third World governments. They are the questions asked from the point of view of workers, the poor, and the peasants of the Third World.

The questions inquire about the consequences of economic development not for increasing gross national product, but for the amount of income that ends up in the pockets of the poorest families; not for attracting international investors, but for making work valuable to the workers; not for growth in production of whatever is profitable, but for producing particular products that enhance the health, sanitary conditions, nourishment, and housing of those who produce them; not for engaging more workers and families in profit-making enterprises whose benefits trickle down to them, but for creating dignified and economically rewarding jobs in which workers gain, rather than lose, control over their fates.

Asking these questions does not imply that every attempt to expand economic activity in the Third World inevitably contradicts the needs and interests of the common people. Indeed the hope is precisely that development of economies and enhancement of people's lives can go hand in hand. But that this will happen cannot be naively presumed. It is something to be created, protected, and guaranteed. Every scheme proposed by the World Bank, the International Monetary Fund, a corporation, or a government for a new plant, rural industry, land reform, road construction, or extraction of oil must be scrutinized by the citizens of developed nations for the impact these projects will have upon the workers who will be affected by them. Will these workers be forced off their land and into factories? Will they earn more money but lose their dignity by being subjected to a harsh work pace unprotected by unions and government regulation? Will they be advancing their families' welfare or will they be producing luxury goods for the rich minority? Will they plant and harvest food to improve their own diets or only to enrich the coffers of local and international exporters?

Too often when we in the First World advocate economic

development as the solution to poverty and underdevelopment we forget that the consequences of economic expansion in the Third World differ dramatically from the consequences of expansion in the First World. In market economies almost all job creation is first and foremost profit creating; it will be carried out, therefore, as ruthlessly as political and moral constraints will allow. Even today job creation in the Third World invariably spawns employment relations akin to those that plagued workers in the United States and Great Britain during the 19th and early 20th centuries when corporations ruled the roost, imposed work regimes on adults and children alike, and otherwise profited from the poverty of the masses by paying low wages, firing dissenters, and refusing to grant workers job security, health benefits, or pensions.

For these, and other reasons discussed below, employment is not a good at any cost. To understand this we must examine what is behind past employment practices in the Third World. We must inquire at every juncture whether there is any reason to hope that more investment—no matter how highly acclaimed by those proposing it—will result in anything more than an extension of subjugation and misery. This has been the case in Brazil, touted as the "economic miracle" among developing market economies. Chomsky and Herman (1977: 33–34) report:

> The relative share of the richest 5 percent increased from 29 percent in 1960 to 38 percent in 1970; the real income of the lowest 40 percent of income-receiving units fell absolutely during the same decade. *Business Week* reported (April 28, 1975) that the real wages of the lowest 80 percent of the Brazilian population have been steadily dropping since 1964—the year the generals took over—despite a tripling of the gross national product to $80 billion. In 1971, 65 percent of Brazil's economically active population subsisted on a monthly income of $60 or less; only 1 percent earned $350 per month and over, but many of these earned $5,000 a month or more. In entire provinces of Brazil the average income is under 10 percent of that of other provinces.

From the beginning three fundamental distinctions need to be made about just what it means to speak of *employment problems in a global perspective.* More will be said about these distinctions later on, but some remarks are in order at the outset since these distinctions define the basic concepts used in all that follows.

First, *employment* is not merely an abstract economic concept, nor is it simply a job someone does. Rather it is a living and changing social *relationship* between those who employ workers and those who are employed. This relationship occurs at the place of work and determines the type of work done, work conditions, job security, promotion opportunities, wages and benefits, work satisfaction, and chances of being fired. Each employment relationship determines these results in a specific way depending on the type of work done, the skill level of the worker, and the pool of resources made available for compensating workers. More basically, however, all the outcomes of the employment relationship derive from the fundamental fact that employment ultimately crystallizes the uneven relationship between employer and employee. The total pattern or distribution of types, numbers, and locations of these uneven employment relationships comprises a society's overall structure of employment. In both advanced and Third World free-enterprise, market economies, the structure of employment, like individual employment relationships, results (with some modification due to worker struggles) from investment decisions by those who hire workers to produce commodities for profit.

Second, the vast array of employment *problems* in the Third World and in the world at large are first and foremost manifestations of a single employment *problem*. Employment problems of unemployment, underemployment, inadequate income, and unfulfilling work are not ultimately plural in nature, even though they may appear to be so. Rather, they result from the basic, underlying fact of the uneven relationship of power between employer and employee. In market economies, unions and various forms of legal regulation may enable workers to counter and constrain some aspects of employer power. But in the end, the entire economic, legal, and cultural system supports the right of employers to hire and fire workers, to determine work procedures, to control investment decisions, to decide on the lines and levels of production, and ultimately to cease employment altogether by closing businesses and moving them to new locations. Individual workers or even whole segments of classes may not experience their employment as entailing this fundamental problem, nor may they necessarily discern any specific employment problems. Nevertheless, the crucial reality is that employment problems in all their historical and personal weight originate from and reflect the fundamental employment problem of domination in the work relationship.

Third, a *global perspective* on employment is not merely just one more or less useful vantage point that may be abandoned in favor of some non-global perspective. Rather a global perspective is a *privileged point of view* because employment itself, its movement from one nation to another, its expansion and crises are in concrete practice and consequence global in nature. But not only is it incorrect to replace a global perspective by one or another non-global perspective, it is crucial that the global perspective reflect the global nature of the dependency, uneven development, and social movements that characterize the reality of employment in the Third World.

I

EMPLOYMENT PROBLEMS IN THE THIRD WORLD

The three decades since World War II have been characterized, according to an ILO (1976:15) report, by "rapid and sustained growth in national output and investment in both developed and developing countries." Nevertheless, all evidence reveals that especially in the non-socialist Third World nations the attempt to curtail poverty and unemployment by policies of high investment have failed. In fact, the economic fortunes of most developing nations have worsened relative to those of the developed nations; and within these Third World countries the brunt of the economic woes continues to be borne by the majority of workers trapped at the bottom rungs of the economic ladder.

Because workers in the Third World receive little or no income from welfare programs, and because those who cannot find employment are able to become self-employed as vendors or merchants in the informal street economy, statistics on unemployment, underemployment, poverty, and income inequality are intricately tied together and only when taken together do they approximate the hardship faced by almost 70% of the population in the Third World.

Unemployment ⌐

The meaning of unemployment in the Third World is not altogether clear, nor is it the case that unemployment statistics necessarily capture the failure of the employment structure as well as data on underemployment. Still, the disconcerting fact is that of a labor force of around 700 million in the developing countries, estimates of unemployment range from 4.7% to over 7.6%. A number of important considerations put these statistics in perspective. First, the numbers of unemployed do not accurately portray the actual number of people who suffer hardship because of unemployment. Each unemployed person represents two to three more dependents who suffer along with the unemployed worker. Thus 33 to 54 million unemployed in the Third World represent 70 to 150 million who are affected by their joblessness. On the other hand, such figures taken alone may overemphasize the hardship faced by the unemployed and their families since the unemployed may not be heads of households and since others in the family are often employed.

Accordingly, the problem of simply being without a job, or what the ILO calls open unemployment, is often less grave in developing than in industrialized countries. The unemployed in developing countries are often youth, those entering the job market for the first time, women, and the relatively better educated (ILO, 1976:17). Despite our preconceptions, strict joblessness 1) does not affect a large fraction of the total labor force and 2) is generally greater in urban rather than rural areas. This is for two reasons. First, joblessness is a function of the structure of advanced sectors where workers are either less inclined or less able to find alternative employment during recessions. Comparing the figures we find that during the post-1973 recession unemployment was 5.2% in developed countries while it was only 4.7% in the developing nations. Second while total unemployment in developing nations was 4.7%, urban unemployment was 8.0%.

Another factor that clarifies the meaning of statistics on unemployment is that the growth of unemployment in developing nations has spurted in recent years. Even from 1960 to the pre-recession year, 1973, unemployment increased by 46%, an average growth of 3% each year. Sabolo warns that "unemployment is growing faster than employment" and that in 1973 unemployment reached the staggering figure of 54 million, equal to the combined active populations of Great Britain and the Federal Republic of Germany (1975:408). Finally, as Sabolo (1975) also shows, things will get worse. His calculations to 1990 show an increasing unemployment rate up to 8.2% for developing countries. He does not calculate comparable predictions for underemployment but it should be clear that underemployment will likewise increase. This should dispel any naive hope for an easy or quick solution to the economic distress of hundreds of millions of workers and their dependents.[1]

Underemployment

To grasp the hardship perpetrated by the inadequacies in the structure of employment, we must examine other aspects of the employment problem in the Third World. For instance, seasonal unemployment often cuts sharply into the ability of workers to earn a living. But most important is the appalling degree of underemployment. Underemployment is defined by the ILO as "persons who are in employment of less than normal duration and who are seeking or would accept additional work and persons with a job yielding inadequate income" (1976:18). Assuming that underemployment reflects each nation's concepts of inadequate income and low levels of productivity, almost 36% of the total labor force suffer underemployment. One estimate is that of the 700 million workers in the Third World, 250 million are underemployed (Sabolo: 408). For instance, in 1973 before the recent world recession, 29% of the work force in the developing nations was either unemployed or underemployed. Furthermore, also using ILO data, by 1975 underemployment alone was almost 36% and the combined unemployment-underemployment rate climbed to over 40%. Although the figures for 1973 and 1975 are calculated in slightly different ways, there is no doubt that it is increasingly difficult for Third World workers to earn subsistence from employment in their market economies.

Poverty

Just as the employment problem in the Third World is manifested in the high rate of underemployment, in turn the crucial human reality associated with underemployment is the grave fact of destitution. Approximately the same proportion of the population classified as underemployed (40%) is also classified as destitute or in acute poverty (39%). This line of acute poverty is calculated by the ILO in such a way as to take account of the differing costs of a typical basket of goods in the various parts of the Third World; if anything, therefore, the figures under-rather than overestimate the dire straits of the majority of people in the Third World.[2] The poverty line of the "destitute" is defined as equivalent to income per head measured in U.S. dollars of $250 in Western Europe, $90 in Latin America, $59 in Africa, and $50 in Asia. The poverty line for the seriously poor is simply double these amounts.

The meaning of these poverty lines as a measure of human suffering can be grasped by noting that the World Food Conference claims that around 1970 at least 460 million people (of whom 50% are young children and of whom 93% live in developing market economies) suffer from a severe degree of protein-energy malnutrition. Again these figures underestimate the problem. As the ILO notes:

These numbers have undoubtedly increased as a result of the difficult world food situation that has developed since 1972. It is estimated that, even if projected increases in the effective demand for food (assuming no measures of income redistribution) can be met, they will increase to 750 million by 1985.

Moreover, the standard of a "severe degree" of protein-energy malnutrition is a very low one, and many more people suffer from some degree of hunger and malnutrition (1976:21, footnote 2).

Still the number of poor defined by the two poverty lines is even greater. In 1972, not only were 706 million people living in destitution (39%), but some 500 million more, totaling over 1,200 million were "seriously poor." This last figure represents a staggering 67% of the population of developing market economies.

Like the underemployed, the number of poor has grown substantially despite the rapid growth rates in most Third World nations. This runs counter to the mainstream view that development ameliorates poverty. Figures show a dramatic increase in poverty from 1963 to 1972.

Calculating the number of seriously poor and destitute in the same manner the ILO reports that "whereas the proportion of the population in each category declined slightly in each region, this was offset by demographic expansion, so that they increased in absolute numbers" (1976:23). Thus in 10 years the seriously poor increased by 119 million and the destitute by 43 million. Also:

If one examines the 32 individual countries for which data are available, it will be found that the number of "destitute" people increased in 17 countries in 1963–72 and the number of persons suffering from "serious poverty" increased in 14. Among other indicators of deprivation, UNESCO estimates that the number of illiterate adults rose from 700 million in 1960 to 760 million in 1970 (ILO, 1976:23).

Inequality

A final indicator of the employment problem in the Third World is the inequality of income. In the absence of substantial welfare payments, unemployment compensation, and widespread ownership of real estate, stocks and bonds, the distribution of income reflects what happens in the employment structure. Workers' incomes reflect their status in the labor market, and the distribution of income reflects in the Third World even more than in the developed nations the relative distribution of the value and power of employment opportunities.

Research on income inequality from both radical and conservative points of view concurs that incomes are more unequally distributed in developing than developed market economies. Although the research is abundant and highly technical and the data often unreliable, the consensus is that: "In most developing countries the richest 10 per cent of households typically receive about 40 percent of personal income whereas the poorest 40 percent receive 15 percent or less, and the poorest 20 percent receive about 5 percent" (ILO, 1976:22). While researchers agree on this general distribution of income in developing economies, they do not agree on the relationship between increased capital investment and the degree of inequality. Descriptively, it is accurate to say that during the process of economic growth income distribution has become more unequal in some countries and more equal in others. But because there have been virtually no data collected on the changes in income distribution for particular nations as they develop, research has been forced to generalize about changes in income distribution during the process of development by comparing income distributions of different countries at different levels of economic growth.

The findings, contrary to the widely maintained belief that economic growth induces betterment for the poor, are 1) during the initial and intermediate stages of development (that is, until per capita incomes reach about $500, a level yet unattainable except by a handful of Third World market economies) the share of income going to the richest 5% increases while the share going to the bottom 40 or 60% declines relatively and often absolutely as well (cf. Adelman and Morris, 1973); and 2) after this point income inequality does decrease but only moderately, and largely through gains accruing to middle income groups rather than to the poorest 20% (cf. Paukert, 1973 and Kuznets, 1963).

As can be seen, the economic woes facing workers in the Third

World are devastating and persistent. And the future promises little more. Population growth should increase the total labor force in developing market economies from 700 million to approximately 1,400 by the end of the century. By the year 2000 over 1 billion new jobs will be needed in the developing market economies to accommodate the 700 million increase in the labor force as well as the 300 million who are presently unemployed or underemployed (cf. ILO, 1976:47).

II
PERSPECTIVES ON THE EMPLOYMENT PROBLEM

Facts and statistics do not tell the whole story of employment problems in the Third World. It is equally important to explain how the realities behind the statistics came into being and why they will persist into the foreseeable future. This requires that two issues be addressed. First, why is the employment relationship in market economies so central, and why does it necessarily entail domination? Second, how is the employment problem in the Third World in fact a global reality? To answer the first question we must trace the essential elements that constitute employment in free-enterprise economies. To answer the second question we must examine the specific way advanced market economies have affected Third World development.

The Nature and Meaning of Employment in Market Economies

The essence of the capitalist manner of employment, which has increasingly supplanted all previous forms since the 17th century, is that workers must sell their ability to work to an employer who then organizes it to produce commodities which are sold for profit. Capitalism is not the first or the only economic system that has organized the labor of workers for gain. What is distinctive is that for the first time those who control labor do so not to directly obtain goods and services which they or their household will use but to sell them for profit. This new profit making order requires that workers can be found who will make goods and services that are worth more on the market than what must be paid them to keep themselves and their families alive. This means that no longer are workers forced to sell or trade just the fruit of their labor to someone else in order to earn a livelihood. Now workers must sell their very ability to work. While some workers remain independent and self-employed, the overall organization of a market economy determines that the vast majority of those who produce goods and services are employed by others. Now all this requires a malleable labor force.

It is not a coincidence that the economic, legal, and coercive forces spawned by the emergence of market relations tear workers from their farms, small shops, and independent craft work. Workers become unable to work for their subsistence unless they place themselves on the auction block at a price low enough to induce an employer to buy their physical and mental capacities. In this dispensation, workers have no alternative but to accept the rules of the game for employment set by employers. These rules, enforced by state power and culture, provide that employers within certain constraints set by worker economic and political organizations and by the supply of workers determine, in the last instance, which and how many workers will be hired, where and how they will work, and with what compensations they will be paid. This is the fundamental social reality that enables us to speak of the employment relationship under capitalism as one of domination of employees by employers. That is, the nature of work is so modified under capitalism that workers are essentially powerless to earn a living outside attachment to an employment position determined by an employer.

Those who produce goods and services do not control either the goal, process, or benefits of that production. Profit is created socially by workers gathered together in integrated and interdependent forms of production, but such production and its subsequent profit are controlled privately by employers. This general relationship of domination by employers over employees permeates each individual employment position as well as the totality of employment positions comprising the employment structure in the total society.[3]

And so on the broadest level, the explanation for the vast array of employment problems plaguing workers in market economies across the world resides ultimately in the domination inherent in the nature of the employment relationship. In these economies profit making firms strive for, and in a structural sense, must strive for enlisting the least number of workers at the lowest possible wages commensurate with profitable production. As a result unemployment, underemployment, poverty, and inequality fill the biographies of millions of workers and their families.

The Global Reality of Employment Structures

But still we must understand just why such plight is extended to its most inhumane proportions in the peripheral, backward economies of the underdeveloped Third World. Why are the consequences of unemployment and poverty played out with such a vengeance in the so-called underdeveloped countries? Why does the structure of employment in underdeveloped countries entail a distribution of types and numbers of jobs so incapable of sustaining the livelihood of vast numbers of workers?

The most widely held explanation for these dire consequences for Third World workers is provided by what is often referred to as development or modernization theory. Proponents of developmentalism are not in full accord on the causes of and remedies for underdevelopment but they do concur that underdevelopment is due to the failure, for whatever reason, of the underdeveloped nation to take up "modern" ways of thought, behavior, and economic structures which are necessary to motivate industrial development, create employment, and decrease poverty.[4] Underdeveloped nations as a whole are simply at the earliest stages along the same path of development experienced by advanced market economies. Internally, underdeveloped nations are dual societies where developed sectors suffer from the drag of more backward sectors. Consequently North American and Western European patterns of culture and behavior must be diffused to underdeveloped nations in general and to the most backward regions and populations within those nations in particular (cf. Lerner, 1958;

Inkeles and Smith, 1974). When and if sufficient doses of capital and technology become administered to the economies of the underdeveloped nations, these nations will undergo their take-off into self-sustained, self-reliant economic growth; general well-being will rise and benefits will trickle down to the masses (cf. Rostow, 1960, 1975). <u>Most succinctly, underdevelopment essentially stems from the lack of penetration of capitalist market relations.</u>

An alternative view argues that <u>underdevelopment derives not from the lack, but from an overdose of capitalist investment and employment.</u>[5] Development and underdevelopment are two sides of the same coin. The development of center economies requires imperialist domination of dependent nations; the development of advanced industrial market economies is simultaneously and necessarily the development of the underdevelopment of the Third World. From the beginning the development of the world capitalist economy was based on the articulation of underdeveloped nations to the economic and political needs of the developed ones. Underdevelopment is not a given initial state of backwardness, a pristine but outmoded economic system that requires modernization; rather it is a process that creates and recreates each phase of development in the advanced countries by the circumstances of underdevelopment in the dependent ones.

There are three general phases of this development of underdevelopment or the development of dependency. The first phase occurred approximately from 1700 until World War I. The earliest stages of this period were characterized by the extraction of precious metals, foodstuffs, slaves, and other resources needed to enhance the early beginnings of market economies in Europe and North America. Later, transportation infrastructures of roads, railroads, communication networks, and ports were extended and organized to meet the needs of the international expansion of trade relations by linking the expanding mining centers and plantations to the world market. Later, the institutional infrastructure of state agencies, banking concerns, and international financing institutions were developed in order to stabilize prices and exchange rates and to encourage foreign financing.

The second phase of penetration of the Third World by market relations began after World War I and continued throughout World War II. This period witnessed the rise of investment in manufacturing known as the epoch of import substitution. International and national investors vied to take advantage of abundant cheap labor to produce goods in the underdeveloped country which were previously imported. Local investors attained their greatest success in forging an indigenous market economy, especially in Brazil, Argentina, and Mexico, during the Great Depression when weakened international investors temporarily lost their dominance. This reprieve from international penetration permitted the formation of a supporting cast of native commercial and financial entrepreneurs and helped spread class and market relations to all sectors of the economy. But the ascendancy of national investors was short-lived. Already faced by competition from the established plantation aristocracy, national investors faced the reemergence of foreign capital after the Depression in mining, manufacturing, and export agriculture. It was during this same period also that international efforts to reduce infant mortality led to accelerated population growth.

The third epoch is the most important from the point of view of these considerations. It began around 1950 and continues to the present. The dire consequences for employment, underemployment, and poverty of the previous stages of the asymmetrical articulation between advanced and dependent economies are played out most fully in this phase. During this period corporations formed conglomerates and monopolies in the advanced nations and, as opportunities for high profitability decreased, expanded their quest for investment and profits in the Third World. Unlike the previous epoch, investment in this third stage was directed not simply toward extraction or toward producing goods for internal consumption. Rather the availability of cheap and abundant labor, less costly and more proximate raw materials, and less restrictive government regulations and taxes induced international manufacturing and finance corporations to begin producing goods in the Third World for international markets as well. The outcome of this series of developments is a segmented economy comprised of 1) capital intensive international capital; 2) more labor intensive national capital; and 3) incompletely capitalized service, agricultural and artisan sectors.

More particularly, the development of underdevelopment of Third World economies in this third stage took the form of four interdependent economic practices: (1) extraction of raw materials and foodstuffs; (2) exporting advanced technology to the Third World; (3) producing products in a Third World country for sale in that nation; and (4) manufacturing products in the Third World for sale on the international market.

At first glance these practices may appear no different from those carried out within and between advanced market economies themselves. The crucial difference is that in the advanced nations these mechanisms developed and expanded their economies in an organic sequence. However, the development of Third World market economies took place from the beginning in the shadow, or better, in accord with the needs of the development of the advanced nations. Consequently, the condition for the linear development of advanced economies was the development of underdevelopment of the Third World.

But what does it mean to say that problems of unemployment, underemployment, and poverty are first a problem of the employment structure, and that the problem of the employment structure is, in turn, a function of the distorted nature of Third World market economies? How did it come about that Third World employment structures are incapable of providing subsistence for the vast majority of their people? Why are there so few job opportunities in which workers are capable of supporting themselves and their families? Why does population increase continue to outstrip growth of decent employment positions? Why do poverty and inequality worsen despite evidence that a more equal distribution of income would produce more independent and balanced development of the Third World? What follows is an outline of the primary aspects of the truncated nature of Third World market economies that produce the series of employment problems plaguing workers in the Third World today and insure that these problems will persist.

1. The most fundamental manifestation and continually re-

created consequence of dependent development is the increasingly skewed distribution of income. As we have seen, the greater the economic development of a dependent market economy, as measured in per-capita income, the greater inequality of income distribution. Regrettably, this has reinforced a pattern of local and international investment that caters to a narrow market demand for luxury and durable goods rather than to the broader market demand for mass consumer goods. Consequently, Third World economies produce an inordinate amount of goods that are manufactured by techniques that require relatively little labor. Mass demand thereby remains low, and the cycle of income inequality, underemployment, and distorted investment priority continues. As Wilber and Weaver (1975:203) complain,

> In a poor country, a highly unequal income distribution means that organ transplant clinics will be built in the capital city *instead* of water purification systems in the villages, automobiles will be produced instead of buses, key clubs set up instead of schools, Coca Cola plants built instead of dairies, etc. Both types of output cannot be produced simultaneously. This is the meaning of a low level of national income.

2. A second factor in the creation of a truncated employment structure is the forced orientation of Third World economies toward export activities (cf. Amin, 1976). The needs and rate of growth of advanced nations determine the types and levels of agricultural and mineral exports from the developing nation. While producers in the dependent nations specialize in meeting particular export needs, finance ministers hope against hope that someday their nation's exports will outstrip their imports and provide capital for generating balanced growth. This can never happen, however. First, because the level of imports of capital goods must remain high if industrial growth is to take place and imports of finished products are required to meet the consumer demands of the wealth. Second, because the level of export income is based on the level of demand from the advanced nations, it is impossible for a dependent economy to "catch up" by rallying resources, integrating its development, and "taking off" into self-sustained growth.

Simply to avoid bankruptcy, to retain international credit, and to meet the interest on its debts, the specialized export sector continues to grow and to make use of the most advanced, low-labor technology. Employment may expand in absolute numbers in the export sector, but in view of population growth and urban migration jobs in this proportionately important sector decline relative to the growth in the labor force. Moreover, since such a high proportion of investment is (and must be) allocated to this capital-intensive sector, resources are diverted from areas of production that would employ more workers.

3. A third and related source of economic distortion that retards employment opportunities is the introduction of capital-intensive advanced technology in manufacturing, construction, and agriculture. In advanced nations, such technology was introduced only after the economy had diversified. In the dependent nations, where investment is directed toward profitability and not organic or cumulative development of the local economy, advanced technology is introduced before and not after a diversified economy is able to provide adequate employment and income for the labor force. Despite various forms of land reform during the past two decades, agricultural holdings have remained concentrated in large haciendas and cooperatives. From the point of view of employment, these estates have introduced labor saving technology even though labor is abundant. Although rural population has decreased as a proportion of total population in the Third World, it continues to grow in absolute numbers. The irony is that per capita agricultural production in Latin America, for instance, still has not grown. Thiesenhusen (1971) reports that according to a U.S. Department of Agriculture study (1970:16), "if the per capita agricultural production from 1957 to 1959 were represented by 100, the 1967 index number would be 103; that for 1968, 100; and the 1969 average, 98." In manufacturing between 1925 and 1960 only slightly more than 5 million of the 23 million people added to the Latin American urban labor force were able to be absorbed. In 1925, 35.4% of the Latin American labor force were employed in manufacturing while in 1960 the percentage dropped to 27.1% (cf. United Nations, 1967:62–3). Or as Barraclough puts it, while manufacturing output in Latin America grew by 140% from 1950 to

1965, manufacturing employment grew by only 45% (1969).

4. A fourth characteristic of underdeveloped employment structures is the over-development of the tertiary or so-called service sector. While the underdevelopment of employment in manufacturing, agriculture, and mining account for the parsimony of highly paid workers, and the lack of demand for mass consumer goods, it is the over-extended development of the service sector that accounts for the vast numbers of underemployed and poor in the work force. In advanced nations between 1820 and 1890 the service and manufacturing sectors expanded at the same time, both drawing workers from agricultural production. Only later, around the turn of the century, after manufacturing diversified and increased its per-capita output, did the service sector expand and employ workers displaced by technology. In the Third World, however, the growth of the tertiary sector did not follow the linear sequence that enabled advanced economies to reduce the proportion of workers in manufacturing without mass impoverishment or permanent recession. Instead, to the degree a Third World economy is integrated and subservient to world investment practices, its industry employs fewer workers than the number of craft workers it disemploys and the number of peasants displaced by advanced technology. Thus, says Amin (1976:241), "urban growth is accompanied in the Third World by an increase, both absolute and relative, in unemployment such as did not occur in the West except during brief periods." Moreover, underemployment and poverty abound for the majority of workers engaged in this service sector. For in the absence of systematic social welfare policies, workers displaced from industry and agriculture, along with virtually every member of their household over 10 years of age, take up low-paying employment as domestics, day-laborers, street-cleaners, bus and taxi drivers, janitors, and government service workers. The United Nations (1966) reports that the number of workers absorbed into such forms of disguised unemployment grew at an annual rate of 8.2% and doubled between 1950 and 1965. Surely the number has more than doubled again during the past 10 years. This has resulted in the growth of the poor marginal population at a rate of 15% each year, 10% greater than the growth of the urban population (cf. OAS, 1967:7–10).

5. Finally, it is important to dispel the myth that the development of distorted employment structures results merely from population pressure. It is, of course, true that population growth, especially when combined with rural to urban migration, exacerbated any tendencies toward underemployment and poverty; but it is just as sure that population pressures do not cause these tendencies. As long as social welfare for the disabled and aged remains scarce, and as long as family subsistence depends on the number of household members who can work, large families will remain a reasonable mechanism for insuring economic security. Neo-malthusian arguments that the problem of underdevelopment is one of over-population ignore the fundamental fact that advanced nations required and thrived on large population increases during their industrial development as evidenced by waves of immigrants absorbed by the rapidly expanding U.S. economy during the 19th and 20th centuries. In fact, a precondition for feeding large industrial populations (rather than simply producing export crops) is a relatively dense rural population with access to land. Similarly, industrialization, when accomplished in an integrated fashion, requires abundant labor. For example industrialization in the advanced nations absorbed very high rates of urban population growth and relied on massive influxes of immigrants from rural areas. In the Third World, however, the capitalization of agriculture and production for export has resulted in most good land being used for export cash crops and cattle grazing rather than for new forms of efficient, labor intensive production of food for mass consumption. Consequently, peasants migrate to urban centers, swelling the ranks of the unemployed and underemployed who seek but cannot find employment in highly capital intensive industry.

III
CONCLUSION

This article has investigated the problem of Third World employment in its global context. We began with a statistical description of the debilitating nature of unemployment, underemployment, poverty, and income inequality in the Third World. We went on to explain these statistics, because to have simply described this plight would have failed the cause of those who suffer so gravely. Facts and figures alone offer little guidance for understanding and transforming the social forces at the root of the employment problem in the Third World. For this reason, we also have explored how the vast array of employment problems in the Third World derive in general from the nature of employment in free-enterprise economies and more particularly from the way Third World employment structures have been distorted over the ages by their asymmetrical, subordinate articulation to investment practices originating in advanced market economies.

Urban industrialization and commercialization of agricultural production are both job-creating and job destroying. Changes in the structure of the labor force which result from new investment lead to a divorce of artisan and peasant producers from direct control over their job activities. World Bank, International Monetary Fund, and private investment policies explicitly or implicitly recommend the destruction of such direct worker control and the creation of a rural wage-labor force as well as a low-wage service sector. Commercialization of agriculture exiles peasants to further hopelessness in the cities where industries, employing high capital-intensive technologies imported from Europe and the U.S. are unable to absorb them. Thus there is, hand in glove, economic growth and deterioration in the quality of life for labor. This often precipitates so much worker dissent and political organization that the established pattern of development can be maintained only through government control and oppression. This is the economic basis for the violation of human rights as we have come to know them in the First World.

In this way the Third World problems of employment are more fundamentally manifestations of the single employment problem of the numbers, types, and distribution of employment opportunities provided by truncated Third World employment structures. In turn, these distorted employment structures result from the structural imbalances introduced into Third World economies by their being developed not autonomously but in an extraverted manner. That is, they are oriented externally to the economic needs and requirements for development of the advanced economies. Consequently, the development of advanced market economies has become simultaneously the development of underdevelopment of Third World economies, the distortion of their employment structures, and the debilitation of hundreds of millions of their people.

NOTES

1. As bleak as these statistics appear, they provide lower estimates of unemployment than proposed by others. Wilber and Weaver (1975:217) summarize a series of studies which paint this gloomier picture: "An OECD study estimated urban unemployment at 15 percent in Ceylon, 14 percent in Columbia, 12 percent in the Philippines, and 21 percent in Guyana (Turnham and Jaeger, 1970). Pakistan's experience of rapid growth also shows unemployment increase each year (Haq, 1971). Hans Singer has recently estimated that unemployment in underdeveloped countries (not counting disguised unemployment) amounts to at least 25 percent of the labor force (Singer, 1971). Turner, in a study of fourteen underdeveloped countries, found unemployment growing at a rate of 8.5% per year (Singer, 1971). The Prebisch Report concluded that for Latin America, GNP would have to grow at a rate of 6 percent per year between 1970 and 1980 just to maintain the unemployment levels of 1960" (Prebisch, 1971).

2. A description of the methodology and its advantages over other means of calculating poverty are given in the ILO report, *Employment Growth and Basic Needs* (1976:20–22).

3. The totality of the number, type, and location of employment positions (the employment structure) is determined by employer/investor decisions. But these employers, of course, are not simplistically acting in concert to ruin workers; cries of conspiracy (even when collusion is in evidence) do not begin to explain how the employment structure is determined. It is true, however, that the employment structure in a society derives from economic decisions made by owners of the means of production and not by those who work in them. These decisions are themselves subject to the exigencies of making profits and the inherent structural requirement that the market value of what is produced outstrip worker benefits and that the employment opportunities offered workers be of a type and with a level of remuneration that do not subvert the advancement of profitability.

4. Writers whose research follows this approach include Rostow (1960, 1975), McClelland (1961), Hoselitz (1960), Lipset (1959, 1976), and Inkeles and Smith (1974). Nash (1963:5) reviews the variations within this

model of development: "There are, in my view, only three modes of attacking the problem of social change and economic development. The first mode is the index method: the general features of a developed economy are abstracted as an ideal type and then contrasted with the equally ideal typical features of a poor economy and society. In this mode, development is viewed as the transformation of one type into the other. . . . The second mode is the acculturation view of the process of development. The West (taken here as the Atlantic community of developed nations and their overseas outliers) diffuses knowledge, skills, organization, values, technology and capital to a poor nation, until over time, its society, culture and personnel become variants of that which made the Atlantic community economically successful. . . . The third mode . . . is the analysis of the process as it is now going on in the so-called underdeveloped nations. This approach leads to a smaller scale hypothesis, to a prospective rather than a retrospective view of social change, to a full accounting of the political, social, and cultural context of development" (as quoted in Frank, 1972: 322–23).

5. Important among theorists who stress the process by which advanced market economies underdevelop dependent ones are Cockcroft, Frank, and Johnson (1972), Frank (1967, 1969, 1972), Dos Santos (1970, 1971), Cardoso (1972, 1973). Frank (in Cockcroft, Frank and Johnson, 1972:321), for instance, roundly criticizes each variety of traditional approaches to development for being "empirically invalid when confronted with reality, theoretically inadequate in terms of its own classical social scientific standards, and policy wise ineffective for pursuing its supposed intentions of promoting the development of the underdeveloped countries." The fact is Third World economies have not been nor are they now capable of simply recapitulating the process of economic growth that led to the apparent splendor of the industrialized West. Economies of the Third World are not independent of forces in the world economy and have been structured from their beginning in line with the needs for investment and profit of Europe and North America. Growth rates have been substantial in the Third World, especially since World War II; but poverty, underemployment, and inequality continue to increase. As the Third World grows, its share of world production decreases rather than increases. As Mandel (1975:69) points out, the Third World's share in world trade declined from approximately 32% in 1950 to approximately 17% in 1970. The ILO (1976:4), summarizing the abundant research on the topic, concludes that "contrary to earlier expectations, the experience of the past two decades has shown that rapid growth of aggregate output does not by itself reduce poverty and inequality or provide sufficient productive employment within acceptable periods of time. . . . It is no longer acceptable in human terms or responsible in political terms to wait several generations for the benefits of development to trickle down until they finally reach the poorest groups."

BIBLIOGRAPHY

Adelman, Irma and Cynthia Morris, *Economic Growth and Social Equity* (Stanford: Stanford University Press, 1973).

Amin, Samir, *Unequal Development: An Essay on the Social Formations of Peripheral Capitalism*, tr. Brian Pearce (New York: Monthly Review Press, 1976).

Barraclough, Solon, "Employment Problems Affecting Latin American Agricultural Development," *FAO Monthly Bulletin of Agricultural Economics and Statistics* 18:1–9, 1969.

Blanchard, Francis, "Introduction," *Employment Growth and Basic Needs: A One-World Problem* (Geneva: International Labour Office, 1976).

Cardoso, F. H., "Dependent Capitalist Development in Latin America," *New Left Review*, 74:83–95, 1972.

———, "Dependency and Development in Latin America," pp. 7–16 in Frank Bonilla and Robert Girling (eds.), *Structures of Dependency* (Stanford: Stanford University Press, 1978).

Chomsky, Noam and Edward S. Herman, "The United States Versus Human Rights in the Third World," *Monthly Review* 29, 3:22–45, 1977.

Cockcroft, James D., Andre Gunder Frank and Dale L. Johnson, *Dependence and Underdevelopment: Latin America's Political Economy* (Garden City, N.Y.: Doubleday, 1972).

Dos Santos, T., "La Crisis de la teoria del desarrollo y las relaciones de dependencia en America Latina," pp. 147–87 in *La Dependencia Politico-Economica de America Latina* (Mexico: Siglo Ventiuno, 1970).

———, "The Structure of Dependency," pp. 225–236 in K. T. Fann and D. C. Hodges (eds.), *Readings in U.S. Imperialism* (Boston: Porter Sargent, 1971).

Frank, Andre Gunder, *Capitalism and Underdevelopment in Latin America: Historical Studies of Chile and Brazil* (New York: Monthly Review Press, 1967).

———, *Latin America: Underdevelopment or Revolution. Essays on the Development of Underdevelopment and the Immediate Enemy* (New York: Modern Reader, 1969).

————*Lumpen-Bourgeoisie and Lumpen-Development: Depen-dence, Class and Politics in Latin America*, tr. Marion Davis Berdecio (New York: Monthly Review Press, 1972).

Haq, Mahbub, "Employment in the 1970's: A New Perspective," *International Development Review* 12. Reprinted in Carles K. Wilber (ed.), *The Political Economy of Development and Underdevelopment* (New York: Random House, 1971 and 1973), pp. 262–272.

Hoselitz, Bert F., *Sociological Factors in Economic Development* (Glencoe: The Free Press, 1960).

Inkeles, Alex and David H. Smith, *Becoming Modern: Individual Changes in Six Developing Countries* (Cambridge: Harvard University Press, 1974).

International Labour Office, *Employment, Growth and Basic Needs: A One-World Problem* (Geneva: International Labour Office, 1976).

Kuznets, S., "Quantitative Aspects of the Economic Growth of Nations: VII. Distribution of Income by Size," *Economic Development and Cultural Change*, January 1963, Part II:1–80.

Lerner, Daniel, *The Passing of Traditional Society: Modernizing the Middle East* (Glencoe: The Free Press, 1958).

Mandel, Ernest, *Late Capitalism*, tr. Joris De Bres (London: New Left Review Editions, 1975).

McClelland, David, *The Achieving Society* (Princeton: Van Nostrand, 1961).

Nash, Manning, "Introduction, Approaches to the Study of Economic Growth," pp. 1–19 in M. Nash and R. Chin (eds), *Psycho-Cultural Facts in Asian Economic Growth: Journal of Social Issues* 29, 1, 1963.

Organization of American States, *Social Aspects of Urban Development* (Washington, D.C., 1967).

Paukert, Felix, "Income Distribution at Different Levels of Development: A Survey of Evidence," *International Labour Review* 108: 97–125, 1973.

Prebisch, Raul, *Change and Development: Latin America's Great Task. Report Submitted to the Inter-American Development Bank* (Washington, D.C., 1971).

Rostow, Walt Whitman, *Stages of Economic Growth: A Non-Communist Manifesto* (Cambridge: Cambridge University Press, 1962).

————, *How It All Began: Origins of the Modern Economy* (New York: McGraw-Hill, 1975).

Sabolo, Yves, "Employment and Unemployment, 1960–90," *International Labour Review* 112: 401–417, 1975.

Singer, Hans, "Employment Problems in Developing Countries," *Manpower and Unemployment Research in Africa* 4, 1:21–35, 1971.

Thiesenhusen, William C., "Latin America's Employment Problem," *Science* 171:868–874, 1971.

Turnham, David and Ingeles Jaeger, "The Employment Problem in Less Developed Countries," *OECD:* December 1970.

United Nations Economic Commission for Latin America, *The Process of Industrial Development in Latin America* (New York: United Nations, 1966).

————, *Economic Survey of Latin America, 1965* (New York: International Publications Service, 1967).

U.S. Department of Agriculture, Economic Research Service, *The Agricultural Situation in the Western Hemisphere, Review of 1969 and Outlook for 1970* (Washington, D.C.: Government Printing Office, 1970).

Wilber, Charles K. and James H. Weaver, "The Role of Income Distribution in the Process of Development," *Economic Analysis and Workers' Management* 9:202–224, 1975.

Employment, Basic Human Needs, and Economic Development

Kenneth P. Jameson and Charles K. Wilber

I

"Development" generally implies that changes in a society are moving it toward the "good society." Writers on development often assume that the question of the nature of a good society is already answered, and so their concern is with solving practical problems by applying their expertise. Closer examination indicates that the good society is usually assumed to be an idealized version of the United States economy which is claimed to provide the greatest possible individually marketed goods and services. This suggests that development can be measured by the level of income or product per person. The focus on growth in per capita income as the *deus ex machina* which will solve all problems is simply a logical extension of this approach.

There can be no question that growth has provided a way out of poverty for millions of people. However, we now know that development cannot be reduced to mean solely economic growth. Many countries—Brazil, Pakistan, Nigeria, even Mexico—have had rapid growth rates of per capita income while at the same time unemployment, inequality, and the level of poverty of the mass of the population have remained unchanged or even increased. A thin upper layer has prospered while the vast majority of the population remains entrapped in the backwaters of underdevelopment. With this realization Dudley Seers (Seers, 1969), Mahbub ul Haq (Haq, 1971, 1973), Ivan Illich (Illich, 1969), and others have questioned the emphasis on chasing the consumption standards of the developed countries via economic growth. Instead they argue for a

124

direct attack on poverty through employment and income redistribution policies. In addition, Denis Goulet (Goulet, 1971) and Paulo Freire (Freire, 1970) argue that development must include "liberation" from oppression—cultural as well as political and economic.

To be sure, economic growth in itself is not the problem. The problem arises from a sole preoccupation with growth in a context of underdevelopment, a context characterized by highly unequal income distribution, large-scale structural unemployment, and so on. In these conditions of underdevelopment a continuation of growth-oriented policies means that programs will be based on the consumption demands of the rich minority, and this in turn means the perpetuation of underdevelopment—mass poverty, unemployment, and inequality. Inequality of incomes means luxury goods industries will be expanded while industries producing traditional basic necessities for the poor majority will be neglected. Reliance on individual consumption demand means automobiles will be produced instead of bikes and buses, washing machines and dryers instead of laundromats, Coca Cola instead of milk. Emphasis on individual, rather than collective consumption means that there will be many more durable consumer goods than is necessary. Individually owned cars, television sets, and lawn mowers that sit idle most of the time take up resources that could better be used to benefit more people by supplying those same consumer durables to all of the people on a collective basis—i.e., public buses, community centers, and so on. In addition, these growth oriented programs mean that the capital required for production is much higher and the labor required much lower, for this is one difference between producing goods the rich use and goods for the poor (Soligo, 1974). In addition, such industries typically rely on capital equipment imported from the rich countries. This costs foreign currency; and since such equipment is designed to reduce the amount of labor used in production, the net result of growth oriented development is to leave the unemployment problem, and thus poverty, unsolved.

It can be argued that this growth oriented strategy for development will work in the underdeveloped countries today just as it worked earlier in Western Europe, North America and Japan.

What appear to us as problems now, existed during the earlier growth process. Capitalist development in Europe led initially to increasing inequality of income, high levels of unemployment, control of savings funds by capitalists who re-invested them to produce luxury goods for themselves.

But the growth oriented theory of economic development stresses that inequality of income is necessary to provide incentives for investment. If self-interested, maximizing individuals are allowed to seek differential rewards for their efforts and risk taking, then income will be maximized. Then (if you are a conservative) the benefits will eventually "trickle down" to the less successful in the form of higher wages; or (if you are a liberal) the state could redistribute the benefits when society is rich enough so that incentives will not be drastically impaired. Unfortunately, the results of these two strategies in underdeveloped countries are not very encouraging.

It is true that the experiences of present day underdeveloped countries are very similar to the experiences of Western countries in the 19th century, but some crucial differences make that experience irrelevant for developing countries today. (1) Today the new consumer goods come in from outside rather than from within the country itself. (2) The technology is also imported and uses more capital and machinery than countries with unemployment can afford. (3) The production units today are monopolistic or oligopolistic and are often owned and controlled by foreign multinational corporations. (4) The unemployment problem is much greater today because of the rapid increases in population. (5) Yesterday's underdeveloped countries didn't have a socialist alternative, whereas today's do have several such models. The example of China is a very powerful force in the underdeveloped world today, for she is a country with a very modest level of per capita income which is feeding, clothing, housing, educating and medically caring for a population of 800 million. No capitalist underdeveloped country is able to meet these basic human needs for all its people. Thus, the socialist alternative has a great appeal to the governments of the many countries where starvation, sickness and illiteracy are still rampant.

II

The direct attack on poverty advocated by Mahbub ul Haq as the alternative to growth oriented development has evolved into what is called the "Basic Human Needs" strategy of development. These "needs" have been formulated differently by various authors but the following five categories of basic needs from the World Employment Conference in June 1976 can provide a good outline (Green, 1976):

1. Basic personal consumption goods and services.
2. Access to basic public services.
3. The infrastructure of social overhead capital and capital goods production necessary for the satisfaction of the first two categories of needs.
4. Employment productive enough to allow output requirements to be met and with an income sufficient for each worker to meet his and his family's basic needs (taking household production of consumption goods into account).
5. Effective mass participation in decision-making as well as implementing processes and the decentralization needed to operate such participation.

The ILO states that "in all countries employment enters into a basic-needs strategy both as a means and as an end. Employment yields an output, it provides an income to the employed, and it gives a person the recognition of being engaged in something worth his while" (ILO, 1977). This paper will follow the lead of the ILO and will examine the employment strategy, but it must be remembered that this is only one among a number of interrelated strategies that must be pursued to achieve basic human needs development. Yet it must be a central concern as Mahbub ul Haq (1970) pointed out:

Employment should become a primary objective of planning and no longer be treated as only a secondary objective. Let a society regard its entire labour force as allocable; over this force its limited capital resources must be spread. Let us reverse the present thinking that, since there is only a fixed amount of capital to be allocated at a particular time, it can employ only a certain part of the labour force, leaving the rest unemployed, to subsist on others as hangers-on or as beggars without any personal income, often suffering from the worst forms of malnutrition and squalor. Instead let us treat the pool of labour as given, at any particular time it must be combined with the existing capital stock irrespective of how low the productivity of labour or capital may be. If physical capital is short, skill formation and organization can replace it in the short run. It is only if we proceed from the goal of full employment, with people doing something useful, even with little doses of capital and organization that we can eradicate some of the worst forms of poverty.

Employment is also seen as crucial when it is considered in relation to the manner people receive income. First, for most people this is the primary way that they can earn the income necessary to fulfill their basic needs. Second, because of the universal absence of social service systems, those who cannot work because they are either too old, too young, or incapacitated mentally or physically must depend upon the income generating ability of the family, village, or other group which sustains them.

Let us examine some of the terms used to help us understand the concept better. It is very important when talking about this central issue that the meaning of "full employment" be specified quite precisely. It would be a mistake to think of it in terms of aggregate levels of employment as we usually do in the case of the advanced industrialized countries. Indeed, the case will be made later that policies designed to lower "unemployment rates" may actually be detrimental when employment is evaluated from the perspective of basic needs.

The first thing that must be realized is that "poor" countries or societies are of their nature highly complex, much more so in certain dimensions than are the advanced countries. In the latter, the process of marketization has gone much further, i.e., people rely for their income on money wages, they purchase their consumer needs in markets, and additionally, many human relations have been altered to fit the demands of monetized behavior. The societies of the poor countries have a far greater amount of subsistence activity where producers operate in markets we would not recognize; relations of exchange that have a high social dimension to them, based perhaps on some form of reciprocity, and which make them seem irrational from our viewpoint; producers of a wide variety of products under sets of conditions which vary substantially across products; or persons who will remain seemingly unemployed for long periods but will then take a type of job that had been long available.

The implication of this complexity is that "employment" cannot be defined in a way that is universally applicable, but it is a much broader construct than would be the case in the United States. Some of its aspects are apparent. Employment should refer to some activity which can generate command over material goods, and full employment should refer to providing the opportunity to exercise this control to the fullest extent possible. Another dimension to this is that the activity should provide enough of a command over goods that the person can meet the basic needs of life specified above.

Why worry about this generality? Basically because the definition of employment will vary substantially depending upon the situation of the person or group about whom we are talking. It has now become common to separate several different components of the poor and to look at their situation separately. The first are the openly employed who will generally be found in urban areas. They would work if they could, but cannot find jobs. They will often have a tendency to move into the highly informal sector of the economy to keep themselves alive, often offering services to relatives who provide them room and board. Thus, although they are the group most easily understood by our usual context, they may behave quite differently from the unemployed of the advanced country, and policies designed to aid them may have to be very different as well. Open unemployment is not generally a large fraction of the total labor force, nor are the statistics of open unemployment any real guide to the extent of overall poverty.

Other dimensions of unemployment in underdeveloped countries are of much greater importance. Seasonal unemployment is often extremely large in the rural sectors of poor countries. In this

situation there are workers who are essential at high labor requirement times such as planting or weeding of crops, but whose
contribution at other times is minimal at best. They would be
affected differently by the various employment strategies which
might be undertaken.

The most widespread and critical problem is simply that many
jobs (especially self-employment) yield an income inadequate for
the employed poor to cover their basic needs. (According to traditional development theory low income implies low productivity.
Thus, underemployment is caused by the low level of total
productivity—i.e., of labor, capital, and natural resources combined.) These persons are classified as underemployed and
make up about 36% of the labor force compared to 5% openly
unemployed. About 80% of the total unemployed and underemployed are located in rural areas. Thus, "the employment problem,
like the poverty problem, is largely a rural phenomenon" (ILO,
1977, p. 17).

The fact that the incomes of the underemployed are inadequate to meet their basic needs does not mean that they are idle
like the openly unemployed. In many cases they are fully occupied,
often in household activity. But the key thing is that if more
productive and better paid work opened up, they would make their
labor available. Thus, the problem is not one of employment,
rather it is one of more productive employment. As many writers
put it, it is a matter of raising the "value of the marginal product" of
low income workers. While this is an important point, it should
certainly not be overdone. For even in advanced capitalist countries, we cannot make the assumption that unemployed persons are
idle; they may be fixing their own home, helping neighbors do the
same, contributing voluntary labor, and so on. Thus, the problem
may just as well be viewed as one of shifting them from an activity
which is valued at a lower amount to one which is valued at a higher
rate. This is not always the same as simply raising their productivity.

We conclude this section with some reasons for the emphasis
on employment as opposed to other approaches to meeting basic
needs. This raises a very difficult area which is partly the intrinsic
worth of work as well as partly the sheer efficacy of this particular

approach to providing for the basic needs of individuals. On the first point it should be realized that work has an importance beyond its ability to earn money. Through it human beings realize themselves and allow capabilities to develop and grow, unless the work is structured in such a fashion that this is made impossible. It is through the structuring of employment that dependency on external factors can best be avoided. It is in this fashion that some of the dependency aspects of the basic needs approach can be avoided and the possibility of positive action on the part of the poor can be facilitated. In this fashion many of the best aspects of real human "development" can be assured. Meeting persons' basic needs can become part of a process of empowerment and realization rather than a process of "integration" where persons are forced by their basic needs to jettison fundamental aspects of their self-definition in order to be able to operate in such a fashion as to attain their basic needs.

This has very definite implications for any employment strategy. The types of jobs created, or the type of independent command over physical goods facilitated by employment creation strategies, have an ethical content which is an important component of basic human needs in itself and, thus, is an integral part of the fifth basic need of participation in decision-making. The next section of the paper will pick up on this theme and examine some aspects of the Brazilian model of development with the sole aim of showing some of the unacceptable aspects of that approach to job creation and full employment.

Before turning to those questions however, one other justification for an employment strategy of basic needs must be indicated. Among the many ways of providing for basic needs, systems operate in ways that result in job creation being one of the most efficient and effective manners of providing persons with command over the resources they need. We understand a great deal about economic activity and how it can be stimulated, and thus we understand a great deal about how this process can be utilized to facilitate the attainment of basic human needs. One cautionary note should be added here, however. Much of that knowledge is about job creation at the macroeconomic level. It cannot immediately be assumed that such efforts will translate directly into worthwhile job creation for those who are most in need, as we shall see from the Brazilian example. So the problem is one that is common to all approaches to basic human needs: the targeting of the employment generating activity to insure its benefits to those for whom the strategy is designed. This is a theme to which we will return in the fourth section of the paper and it is perhaps the crucial one when we come to talk about a basic needs strategy which is pursued through the creation of "employment."

III

Brazil's economic accomplishments in the last 10 years are by now well-known and widely debated. In terms of growth in the output of goods and services, the record is fantastic: a doubling of output in the years 1968 to 1974. One of the interesting aspects of the Brazilian case for our purposes is that it was implicitly an employment creation strategy, the view being that stimulation of overall economic activity would create jobs and thereby provide incomes to persons so that their welfare would increase.

One of the criticisms of the Brazilian model has been its effect on the distribution of income in the country. The data for 1960 and 1970 indicate that the share of income going to the wealthiest 10% of the population increased from 40% to 48% over the period, while that for the lowest 40% actually fell from 11% to 9%. Defenders of the Brazilian model have pointed out a number of difficulties with this analysis. The defense which looks at the employment creation effects of the Brazilian model is one of the most interesting for our purposes.

In this case it is pointed out that the number of jobs created in the economy far outran the growth in population, thus implying that persons who did not have jobs before and were poor as a result were able to find jobs as a result of the growth in the economy. Thus goes the claim, the income distribution figures are misleading and the status of the poor improved substantially, i.e., this job creation strategy was effective in meeting basic human needs. Let us examine these claims.

It is helpful to realize once again that jobs in Brazilian terms are wage earning jobs in the modern sector, the monetized sector of the economy. Those who had no "jobs" before were not simply sitting around idle, they may have been in the informal sector or in the rural area in non-wage earning activities. Thus one impact of the Brazilian approach has been to bring more persons into the modern sector wage labor force. There are two interpretations which are possible about this. The first, favorable to Brazil, is that the miracle opened up job possibilities to persons who simply had not had them before thus enabling them to participate—and certainly this is partially true.

An alternative interpretation is that many persons were forced into the modern sector because of changes in the economy: ejection from share-cropped lands in the Northeast; closing down of informal sector activity by government power; removal of slum dwelling places from the city which resulted in necessary reliance on costly transport and therefore on earning income to pay for the transport. In this view, instead of having their earnings and productivity raised in jobs they would like, people were forced out of their accustomed lives and pushed into what were often hard, unfulfilling and not very remunerative employment.

There is substantial evidence to support this view. It apparently costs more hours of work at the minimum wage to attain a living diet: 3¾ hours in 1960 and 8½ hours in 1971. The average workday in many parts of Brazil has risen to 12 hours as people have to work more to live. Davis (1977) has provided many examples of the degradation of the Indian way of life and some examples of virtual genocide in the name of progress for Brazil. He also summarizes evidence on the development of debt servitude in many jungle areas where persons brought in from other regions are turned into virtual slaves by this new system of economic activity.

Aside from the detrimental impact which this type of job creation had on many segments of the Brazilian populace, another of its aspects is notable in light of a basic needs strategy. As Morley (1976) puts it: ". . . the economy was creating a substantial number of very well-paying jobs at the top, thus exacerbating wage differentials, and an already unequal distribution of income," i.e., that many of the jobs have gone to technicians whose salary scales are astronomical. Thus it is this group which has benefited most directly from the Brazilian approach to job creation, and it is this concentration of benefits which has resulted in greater income inequality in the process of the miracle. As a result, high percentages of the workforce have nutritional deficiencies, and infant mortality in San Paulo has actually risen from 62.9 in 1960 to 93 in 1973.

The lesson from this experience should be clear. While the accomplishments of the Brazilian model were substantial and there can be no denial that "jobs" were created for many lower income persons, it incorporates substantial shortcomings if meeting basic human needs is the goal of policy. For in very many cases the ability of groups to meet their basic human needs was impaired, and the main beneficiaries of the Brazilian approach were the higher income technicians. The lesson is that an employment based strategy must target its beneficiaries very carefully. It cannot be one which, in Jack Gurley's words "builds on the best"; rather it must build on the base of the activity and potential of those who are most in need of the fruits of development, of those whose basic human needs are not being met.

IV

One conclusion of this discussion is that policy which relies on *one* strategy as *the* strategy of job and income production is destined to fail. The problems of employment are complex and depend upon the peculiar situations of the individuals involved and on the organization of the particular economy. The usual macroeconomic canons of increasing aggregate demand and monitoring growth of the money supply assume away the complexities of underdeveloped countries and, thus, are at best irrelevant to the problem and at worst can exacerbate the severity of the situation of the poor as in Brazil. In analyzing the applicability of macroeconomic models Todaro points out that:

In most Third World countries, the major bottleneck to higher output and employment levels typically is not insufficient demand but structural and institutional constraints on the supply side. Shortages of capital, raw materials, intermediate products, skilled and managerial human resources, combined with poorly functioning and inefficiently organized commodity and loan markets, poor transport and communications, shortages of foreign exchange and import-dominated consumption patterns among the rich—all of these, and many other structural and institutional factors mitigate against the simple notion that expanded government and private demand will be effective measures to solve employment (and poverty) problems in most Third World countries (Todaro, 1977, p. 178).

The foundation of any employment strategy is that it must of necessity be rural based and oriented. The reasons for this are quite direct. First, in general a very high proportion of the population, especially the poor population of underdeveloped countries, lives and depends for its livelihood on the rural area. Eicher's study of Africa (1977) found that between 50 and 90% of the people lived in areas defined as rural in most common definitions. In Latin America the percentage is probably somewhat lower though it will generally run between 50 and 75%, while in Asia the percentage of people living in rural areas is more comparable to Africa's. Further, the ILO figures indicate that about 80% of the total unemployed and underemployed reside in rural areas.

A second consideration is that many of the persons who live in urban areas have come from the rural sector and still maintain links with it. A World Bank study found that in recent years between one-third and three-fourths of the population increase in a number of the world's major cities came from rural to urban migration. As a result, changes in the rural area will have a direct effect on the urban, and so meeting basic needs in the rural area relates directly to solving the problems of the urban areas. Attempts to fight unemployment only in urban areas will merely trigger migration from the rural areas. Some estimates (Todaro, 1977) indicate that the creation of one urban job induces three job-seekers to migrate from the country. The result is an increase in open unemployment in the urban area and a loss of the output produced by the previously underemployed workers who migrated.

Given this context, what can be said about a strategy for targeting employment opportunities to the rural poor? Such a strategy has a number of major component parts which must be taken into account and dealt with in a very direct and specific fashion.

1. It is the consensus of opinion among observers that in the rural areas of developing countries there is little evidence of purely surplus labor—labor that could be removed from production with no decline in output. Rather the problem is one of labor utilization, for there are significant amounts of seasonal unemployment and underemployment of self-employed farmers, tenants, and hired agricultural workers.

Certainly the shortage of capital and land is a factor in this underemployment. But of even greater importance is the prevailing institutional structure of agriculture. In Latin America the dominance of large landed estates and in Africa and Asia the lack of cooperative structures among the small holdings lead to an extreme underutilization of labor. This situation means that an employment strategy must deal with the issue of land reform. As Raup says: "Wherever there is surplus agricultural labour and shortage of working capital the task of the land tenure system is to put people to work. This is when proposals for land distribution are most strongly compelling" (Raup, 1967).

The evidence is quite clear that a system of small farms can absorb more labor than a large farm system. However, institutions must be developed to enable cooperation in the use of available labor to construct buildings, drainage ditches, fences, maintenance of irrigation systems, reforestation, and so on. As Dorner and Kanel point out ". . . a reorganization of a large farm system on cooperative or communitarian principles can be designed to assure both labour absorption and efficiency in the use of capital" (Dorner and Kanel, 1971). In both the Soviet Union and China the collective farm served as a convenient organizational framework for the mobilization of available labor on capital formation projects such as irrigation canals, reforestation, and so on (Wilber, 1969). For example, in the Soviet Union the work-year per person at work in agriculture was lengthened from around 120 days to approximately 185 days. This was accomplished by having farm operations in the off season handled by just part of the farmers, each continuing to work full time, instead of all the farmers working a few hours each. The labor of the released farmers was then utilized in capital formation. The same process was followed, with better results, in China.

Every developing country must deal with the problem of institutional reform if its rural employment policies are going to work. Some way must be found to institutionalize the conversion of underemployed labor into capital formation.

(2) One obvious factor which affects the situation of rural producers is the price at which they sell their produce. In many countries, the government has a pricing policy which affects or may control this price, and if this influence is exerted to raise the price received, then the rural producer will receive a higher income. This of course is another area where there is a linkage between the urban and the rural sectors, for the prices received by the farmers will obviously affect the prices paid by the urban consumer. A similar case can be made for the inputs into production. To the extent that their prices are set, they will affect the returns to be gained from agriculture and thus can affect the benefits reaped from rural employment.

(3) The technology to be used must be appropriate. In many countries economic policy causes the price of imported capital equipment to be relatively low, thus giving producers an incentive to use machinery rather than labor. The result is that "large tractors and combines dot the rural landscape of Asia, Africa and Latin America while people watch idly by" (Todaro, 1977, p. 183).

In societies which have a surplus of labor at certain periods, it is essential to meeting basic needs that machinery be used only in a fashion which will complement the usage of this labor. In certain cases, machinery can remove the bottleneck of labor at crucial points and thus allow the farming of additional land or the attainment of better yields on the land already farmed. Similar considerations exist for the biological technologies. There are a wide variety of biological processes which vary over different types of products and in different growing situations. They require different types of care and different types of water or fertilizer, all of which have implications for labor use and for returns to production. Once again these factors can be manipulated in such a fashion that they benefit the producer.

The choice of inappropriate technology is not the result solely of improper pricing policies such as favorable foreign exchange rates for the importation of agricultural machinery. Institutional factors, such as land tenure, also play an important role. For example, in Latin America the existing distribution of land results in a gross misallocation of resources given the relative availability of land, labor and capital. The large farms use too much land and capital and too little labor while the small farms use too much labor and too little land and capital. "In Latin America, 30-40 percent of the active agricultural population typically lives on and works less than 10 percent of the land" (Dorner and Kanel, 1971). Making more land available through land reform and more capital through improved credit facilities would increase both labor and total productivity.

Large farms underutilize labor and use inappropriate technologies for a variety of reasons. Given the extremely large scale of some farms in Latin America, for example, it would be difficult to manage a large unskilled labor force in a labor-intensive operation. In addition, there would be increased risk in using expensive machinery, improved livestock, and other modern practices that require higher skill levels among the labor force. As a result many large landowners use capital-intensive production methods that require a small but skilled crew of workers. A land reform which reduced the scale of the largest holdings would increase the use of labor per unit of land.

A final issue regarding the appropriateness of technology is the dependency of underdeveloped countries on developed countries for all their machinery and equipment, most of which is labor saving. In the long run poor countries must develop their own indigenous technological research and expand their adaptation capacities.

(4) One of the areas where indigenous technology must be developed is in the provision of rural infrastructure. In many cases the basic infrastructure of roads, water, and so on, some of which are actually components of basic needs, is poorly developed if developed at all. This infrastructure is a crucial component of rural

development because it increases the productivity of rural activity. In addition, such projects can be a major source of employment opportunities so effort must be given to developing low-cost, labor-intensive methods of providing rural infrastructure needs such as irrigation and drainage networks, roads, water supplies, and basic health and education service.

An important by-product of providing these services and amenities is the effect which it should have on migration, i.e., providing an incentive to stay in the rural area rather than moving to the urban centers. Of course this latter decision is highly complex and the experience of the last decades is unlikely to be continued, but it is a crucially important one.

(5) An effort must be made to bring small-scale industry to the countryside. Here again, indigenous development of appropriate technologies that make the fullest use of the local raw materials and labor supply is absolutely crucial in fulfilling the basic needs of the population. Government loans, easier credit, and technical help are all important. A policy of income redistribution from the urban rich to the rural poor would create a market for the types of products easily produced in small-scale, rural industries.

The urban unemployed or underemployed must also be aided in any employment strategy. There seem to be three main areas in which their basic needs can be provided. One is public employment programs; such programs have had substantial impact in the developed countries in terms of avoiding the wastage of human resources in downturns. But as a long run solution, they are flawed for their actual operation in underdeveloped countries has resulted in the creation of a relatively high wage sector with the ability to bring pressure on the central government and thereby frustrate the overall goals of meeting basic needs. When this occurred in Tanzania, the differentials between public service employees and the rest of the society could only be limited by specific controls on public employee salaries.

A second area of importance is the "informal" sector of these economies: the small scale artisans, the small scale service workers such as tailors, shopkeepers, transport workers, and so on. Once again it is quite apparent that government policy has generally favored the modern sector of large scale, hierarchically organized business firms. They are more able to move through the maze of government regulations, circumventing them if they wish to or changing them if they must. Changes in governmental policy which at least provide some flexibility and potential for small scale entrepreneurs would be highly beneficial to providing employment and thus basic human needs.

The third area of importance in the cities is modern industry. For better or worse this sector is destined to be the fastest growing component of the economy. And it is this sector which is the most capital-intensive and labor-saving. Special efforts must be given to employment policies in this sector.

It is often argued in traditional economic writings that since, virtually by definition, there is a shortage of capital and a surplus of labor in underdeveloped countries, labor-intensive techniques should be used wherever possible so as to conserve on capital and provide as much employment as possible. But, to a large degree, this is a false issue. The decision on the type of technology to use cannot be divorced from the decision regarding the allocation of investment. Once the allocation of investment to sectors and industries has been decided the choice of technologies is severely limited. The range of processes available for the production of steel, electric power, tractors, and machine tools is not a continuum where capital and labor are substitutable for each other in very small increments. More realistically, production techniques in these key industries are sharply discontinuous with perhaps two or three viable alternative processes. Further, many of the most modern technologies tend to be both labor and capital saving, as witnessed by the experience of the advanced countries during their industrialization.

Wholesale borrowing of advanced technologies that are labor-saving but not capital-saving would be desirable, however, only if the capital-labor proportions in the underdeveloped country were somewhere near those in the developed country. This is seldom the case. Where this is not the case, redesigning and adapting the most advanced technology to its own capital-labor proportions will yield a larger output.

Adoption of a strategy of a "dual technology" can allow the modern industrial sector to gain the benefits of advanced technology while at the same time greatly expanding employment opportunities. The advanced technologies of the rich countries can be made more appropriate by utilizing manual labor in auxiliary operations and by aiming at high performance rates per unit of capital instead of per man. Between the 1930s and the 1960s the Soviet Union used this strategy with great success.

In many Soviet plants it was common to find the most advanced capital equipment in the basic processes and, at the same time, the most primitive labor-intensive methods in maintenance, intra-plant transport, materials handling and other plant services. In such enterprises as the Gorky Automotive Plant, which in its essentials was a direct copy of the Ford River-Rouge Plant, they allowed for their lower level of labor skills by redesigning job descriptions so that each worker performed fewer and simpler tasks. Thus, the Soviet planners obtained the advantages of advanced technology, conserved scarce capital in auxiliary operations that did not limit output, and utilized their relatively abundant unskilled labor.

Admittedly, a strategy of a "dual technology" is easier to pursue in a socialized economy but it is not impossible for government to use a system of taxes and subsidies to induce private firms to adopt the strategy.

A related feature of this strategy of a "dual technology" was the Soviets' stress upon vocational and technical training and the use of the factory itself in the educational process.

The initial labor force for the plants which opened in the late 1920s and early 1930s was largeiy drawn from peasant and urban youths who had no background or legacy of skills and it was unavoidable that the Soviet Union should develop extensive training facilities. Many of these raw recruits could neither read nor write and had never held a wrench or screwdriver in their hands before. With such raw human material to work with, the plants initially were required not only to train workers to handle their machines and to conform to the factory regime but also to provide the rudiments of an elementary education. As a result, extensive educational and training programmes were established at the factories themselves.

Most of the training was on-the-job in character, but numerous schools known as FZU (factory and works apprentices' schools) were opened at places of work to train apprentices for skilled trades. Also many workers learned their "three R's" in factory run evening schools.

The advantage of on-the-job training, particularly during the early industrialization period, is that it conserves scarce resources. The use of scarce capital in constructing special educational facilities is minimized. In addition the educational gestation period is shortened since the full range of subjects of a normal school is not covered. If the quality of educational output is not high, at least the training is wasteful only of the relatively abundant factor of unskilled labor. In the 1930s on-the-job training was combined with a major over-staffing of the jobs in the factories. While this was "wasteful" of labor, it did have great educational value. This over-staffing combined with the usage of advanced technology was a stimulus to the creation of an industrial work force.

Again, this policy of over-staffing and on-the-job training would be difficult to implement in an underdeveloped country with a capitalist economy because of the non-appropriability of the social benefits by private firms. It is possible, however, that a tax-subsidy scheme could be devised to make the policy feasible.

With this we have a series of policy components which, when utilized jointly, have the potential for a successful "employment strategy" which will aid in meeting the basic human needs of citizens of developing countries.

An employment strategy must be incorporated in an overall development program that includes policies to redistribute income and assets, to provide for integrated rural development, and to control the operation of domestic and international corporations to name only a few of the necessary policies.

Nonetheless, we should reiterate that taking employment as a focus and organizing principle can be highly useful in any strategy of meeting basic needs. Employment is a central component in obtaining the resources necessary to meet basic needs and employment creation is a process about which we have a good deal of understanding.

BIBLIOGRAPHY

Davis, S., *Victims of the Miracle: Development and the Indians of Brazil* (Cambridge University Press, 1977).

Dorner, Peter and Don Kanel, "The Economic Case for Land Reform: Employment, Income Distribution and Productivity," in *Land Reform, Land Settlement and Cooperatives* (Food and Agriculture Organization, 1971).

Eicher, Carl, "Rural Employment in Tropical Africa: Summary of Findings," *Working Paper No. 20, African Rural Economy Program* (Michigan State University, 1977).

Freire, Paulo, *Pedagogy of the Oppressed* (Herder and Herder, 1972).

Goulet, Denis, "An Ethical Model for the Study of Values," *Harvard Education Review* (May 1971).

————, "Development . . . or Liberation?" *International Development Review*, Vol. XII, No. 3 (September 1971). Reprinted in Charles K. Wilber (ed.), *The Political Economy of Development and Underdevelopment* (Random House, 1973).

Green, Reginald H., "World Employment (Geneva, June): Employment, Growth and Basic Needs," *Development Dialogue* (1976:1).

Haq, Mahbub ul, "Employment in the 1970's: A New Perspective," *International Development Review*, Vol. XII, No. 4. Reprinted in Charles K. Wilber (ed.), *The Political Economy of Development and Underdevelopment* (Random House, 1973).

Illich, Ivan, "Outwitting the 'Developed' Countries," in *Celebration of Awareness* (Doubleday, 1969). Reprinted in Charles K. Wilber (ed.), *The Political Economy of Development and Underdevelopment* (Random House, 1973).

International Labour Organization, *Employment, Growth and Basic Needs: A One-World Problem* (Praeger Publishers, 1977).

Morley, Samuel, "Changes in Employment and the Distribution of Income During the Brazilian 'Miracle,' " Mimeo (Vanderbilt University, 1976).

Raup, P. M., "Land Reform and Agricultural Development," in *Agricultural Development and Economic Growth*, H. M. Southworth and B. F. Johnston (eds.) (Cornell University Press, 1967).

Seers, Dudley, "The Meaning of Development," *International Development Review*, Vol. XI, No. 4 (December, 1969). Reprinted in Charles K. Wilber (ed.), *The Political Economy of Development and Underdevelopment* (Random House, 1973).

Todaro, Michael, *Economic Development in the Third World* (Longman, 1977).

Wilber, Charles K., *The Soviet Model and Underdeveloped Countries* (University of North Carolina Press, 1969).

Discussion Questions

1. What are the external forces that have influenced the nature of Third World economies? What are the consequences of Third World economies being built to meet the needs of investors in the advanced economies? What specific internal forces have contributed to the lack of well-paying and personally rewarding employment?

2. Is it true that problems of unemployment, underemployment, poverty and inequality can be viewed as natural outcomes of what Schervish calls the development of underdevelopment? What is this process and how does it differ from more optimistic modernization and development theories? Which of the two approaches better explains the continued employment problems in the Third World and the inability of growth to produce benefits for the majority of the population?

3. What are the questions from the point of view of the poor that must be asked when proposals for economic growth are made?

4. A major theme of Schervish is that previous attempts to develop Third World economies by free-market approaches have not cured but have perpetuated problems of poverty and underemployment. Is there any reason to hope that more investments in the future will produce anything different? What are the major questions to be asked of more hopeful analyses expressed in other chapters? What regulations would you require investors to meet in order to insure that workers gain rather than lose the possibility of fulfilling their basic human need for dignity in their work lives?

5. In a society such as the United States, employment is only one among many competing goals. Jameson and Wilber seem to be suggesting that in underdeveloped countries employment is fundamental and should be a primary goal of those societies. Why do you think there is such a difference in emphasis?

6. While most developed countries have a very low proportion of their population in rural areas working as farmers, Jameson and Wilber suggest that a rural focus is essential for any successful "basic needs" strategy in underdeveloped countries. Why is there such a rural emphasis and what does this mean for any program attempted?

7. According to Jameson and Wilber Brazil was both a success and a failure. In what ways was it a success? What lessons for a basic needs approach can be gained from its failure?

8. What are some of the important components of a rural employment based strategy of growth and equity?

9. How does this strategy relate to the concerns in the other articles, e.g., Paul Streeten's, Denis Goulet's, Albert Waterston's?

V
International Institutions
and a New
International Order Perspective

Multinationals and Development

Richard J. Barnet

Debates about the impact of multinational corporations on developing countries usually break down because the debaters share no common agreement on goals and values—except, perhaps, at dizzying heights of abstraction. The familiar case against the role of the multinationals in developing countries is easily summarized. Global corporations exploit their superior bargaining power in weak, disorganized societies to carry out a series of activities which can offer exceptionally high profits for the world-wide enterprise but which often promote economic and social backwardness in poor countries: The manipulation of transfer prices rob the countries of foreign exchange and reasonable earnings from exports. The technology transferred by multinationals, which is usually designed for the home market in a developed society, is inappropriate to the needs of poor countries. It often displaces jobs and is overpriced. The products manufactured in poor countries are beyond the reach of a majority of the people who lack the money to buy them. Such products are consumed by local elites in enclaves of affluence or they are exported. The export-led model of development of which the multinational corporation has been the principal engine has meant crippling debt and increasing dependence on the rich countries, their private banks and the international lending agencies which they control. Because of their superior control over capital, technology, and marketing global corporations can dominate local economies and preempt the power to plan for the society.

The development model that emerges by default when the global corporation assumes control of the commanding heights of the economy is a highly inequitable one. The gap between rich and poor increases and the bottom 20% of the society appears to be worse off in terms of having its basic needs met than before the development process began. Multinational corporations exert political influence in weak and disorganized societies, and they exert that influence in favor of rightist regimes which are committed to social and economic relationships that preserve inequalities.

The defenders of multinationals, like Senator Daniel P. Moynihan, who think that the global corporations are arguably the "most creative" institutions of our time, minimize these negative consequences. Sometimes company policies have anti-social effects, they say, but it is impossible to generalize. Some corporations help development, others hurt. Besides the countries are becoming effective in limiting the power of multinationals and in bargaining for a greater share of earnings. The evidence is inconclusive about the effects of transfer pricing, technology transfers, etc., and the products offered by the multinationals, while they may not be the best way to meet basic needs, are what people want. Whatever the excesses of the global corporations in the past, these will largely disappear as poor countries become more sophisticated, codes of conduct are enacted, and the companies themselves retrench in their drive to integrate the Third World into the global market.

The defense of multinationals in the Third World usually includes some form of counter-attack. The host countries are confused about their own goals; therefore the multinationals cannot complement them. Their officials are corrupt and self-seeking; the multinationals cannot be blamed if the moral climate is so lax that all successful businesses must bribe in order to survive. Nationalist politicians with their unrealistic chauvinist prescriptions for national development and greedy local entrepreneurs do far more harm to the economy and promote more injustice than the multinationals.

And so on it goes. Studies and counter-studies are hurled back and forth. A few years ago the death of the nation-state at the hands of the multinational corporation was prematurely announced. Now, according to a recent *Fortune* magazine article it is the multinationals that are headed for the ashcan of history—or at least all but a few giants. Despite the confusing war of the studies, enough evidence exists to question Sanford Rose's recent assertion in *Fortune* that multinationals are "marvelously efficient engines of global economic growth and prosperity" if the prosperity we are talking about is the prosperity of the majority. Nor is the multinational corporation particularly efficient, if we take as our criterion conservation of exhaustible natural resources. Multinationals have been engines of certain kinds of growth but not others.

To advance the debate about multinationals and development and to clarify the real choices facing developing countries it is necessary to integrate the multitude of specific findings— economic impacts, social impacts, cultural and political impacts—into a serviceable theory to replace the simpleminded theory of comparative advantage on which most of the conventional euphoric analysis of the global corporation still rests. Elements of such a theory exist. Dependency theory developed by Osvaldo Sunkel and others has been refined into a sophisticated and useful analysis. The process of transnationalization in which capital, labor markets, and culture are increasingly being integrated across national boundaries is now being more systematically studied. The clash of a global urbanization process and subsistence agricultural societies is better understood. But we do not have a way of looking at the global transformation of the world political economy in a holistic way that relates the parts to one another.

To lift the debate about capitalism, industrialization, and development above the level of public relations handouts, lawyer's briefs and demagogic speeches we need to transcend questions about whether multinationals are more or less progressive than national firms or whether they or the local politicians are more to blame for the coexistence of mass poverty and corporate prosperity. All three, multinationals, national firms, and local politicians, are part of a single system of which the multinationals are clearly the most dynamic element. We can begin the process of looking at the multinationals as part of a global system by asking a few basic questions.

The first task is to define what we mean by progressive development and to ask what is the role of the multinationals in that model of development. If we take as the development priority the requirement that minimum basic needs in food, shelter, health, water, and education must be met early in the development process, then the contribution of the multinationals based on the record is almost certain to be negative. By and large multinationals do not make products that are designed for the poorest 60% of the population. They are not in the business of producing low-cost housing, cheap food, village medical care, or "appropriate" technology. If one were to make an inventory of "basic needs" on the left side of the page and a list of the products of the multinationals on the right side, the result would be an almost perfect misfit. The same result, by the way, holds for developed societies too. If one were to make an inventory of the most obvious national needs for the United States—the elimination of substandard housing, distribution of medical care, elimination of malnutrition, rebuilding inner cities, cleaning rivers, environmental protection, development of cheap and efficient energy—one could not expect the multinationals with their present basket of goods to meet these needs.

The reason why multinationals are unable to meet basic needs of the poor is that by and large there is no market for them. What Osvaldo Sunkel calls the "structural heterogeneity" of underdeveloped societies constitutes an economic and social reality that bears little resemblance to the model of the market in neoclassical economic theory. A complex of power structures, as he calls them, explains what economists like to call "market imperfections":

The differences in standards of living among the different sectors of the population . . . are due, to a great extent . . . to the differences of power which exist among the different classes and social groups (white-collar workers, professionals and technicians, employees, labourers) within a given economic activity; to the differences in power which exist among sectors of economic activity (agriculture vs. industry, exporters vs. importers, foreign vs. national firms, large entrepreneurs vs. medium sized or small ones); to regional differences in power, etc. By means of these power relations, which to a large extent determine prices, wages, taxes, tariffs, distribution of public expenditure, of credits, etc., a complex network of income transfers between the various activities, regions, and groups and social classes is produced which explains the lack of correspondence between the level of productivity of a person and his standard of living.

Mere adjustment of economic policies, therefore, cannot make the market work to meet basic needs. The distribution of political power in developing countries is such that money does not find its way to the poor to enable them to buy basic goods and services. The multinational corporation, like any other profit-making institution, operates under a narrow set of goals—profit maximization, long-term stability, and growth. Its purpose is obviously not redistribution of income or meeting basic needs for which there is no market. The larger the corporation, the more global and integrated its operations, the less dependent it is on the government in any one territory in which it operates, the less it is likely to be sensitive to the welfare of people in that territory. A New York corporation with the task of maximizing its global profits, and more especially, of showing the most attractive possible quarterly statement to the shareholders, is not going to forego opportunities for quick profits in poor countries unless power relations force it to modify or to compromise its traditional goals.

This brings us then to the second question: What is the power of the state in developing countries to force multinationals to modify their goals? Corporate spokesmen who are aware that the exercise of power of the multinational corporations for which they are not held accountable raises the most serious challenge to their legitimacy, like to point out that even the tiniest sovereign can nationalize all the assets on its territory of the mightiest industrial giant. From that ultimate power other lesser powers flow—the power to oversee the activities of the corporation, to keep striking ever more favorable bargains, to extract more earnings, etc.

Compared with periods of colonial exploitation or even with the 1950s and 1960s, before developing countries became conscious of transfer pricing, the terms of technology transfer, and related issues and before there was even a semblance of solidarity among the poor countries, the bargaining relationship between developing countries' governments and multinational corporations is less unequal. But except for a few oil-producing nations the governments of poor countries are no match for the multinational corporations. (Even here the big oil companies have done very well. As W. E. Lindenmuth, general manager of the Middle East Department at Mobil, puts it ". . . the Saudis realize that they need us more today than they did five or ten years ago.") Despite the shocking statistics on transfer pricing that have been widely documented in many studies, the problems of obtaining the necessary information to police these exploitative practices have yet to be solved. Multinationals are, as corporate spokesmen like to point out, "whipping boys" in international forums and in domestic political speeches, but the speeches do not change the power relationships.

The power multinational corporations are able to exercise over governments of developing nations is derived from their control over capital, technology, and markets but, most importantly, from their ideology. The multinationals are the only available instrument, so it is widely believed, for achieving the model of development developing countries want: This belief that there is essentially one model of development, the one through which the industrial nations of Europe, the United States, and Japan passed, is the trump card of the multinational corporation. Any nation, whatever its internal social and economic system, that sees the path to progress in the familiar terms—building up urban industrial centers, sacrificing agriculture, importing technology, integrating the local economy into the world economy on whatever terms possible—is permanently dependent upon foreign capital, and because of that dependence its bargaining power is limited.

To be sure, the multinationals now face constraints that were not evident in the years of rapid expansion of their global operations. The shift of world production to the Southern hemisphere to take advantage of cheap labor was premised on cheap transportation costs and healthy growth in the world economy. Neither can be assumed in the present period. Many multinationals face mounting troubles because of growing political instability around the world, the growth of protectionism, the rise of tension among the industrialized countries, and the loss of some control over the costs of resources. However, these difficulties are not usually translatable into bargaining power for poor countries. If a developing country seeks to impose conditions on its operations that seem burdensome to a corporation, it can leave. If the host government fails to provide a good investment climate because it is trying to change the traditional terms of doing business, the certain result, except where the country commands some vital natural resource, is a flight of capital. The recent moderation of the Andean Pact, for example, which in the early 1970s seemed committed to far-reaching measures for changing the relationship between the multinationals and host governments, reflects the conservative governments that have come to power in Latin America and a new awareness that the room to maneuver for countries integrated into the international capitalist economy is limited.

Given the reality that the power to control multinationals is limited, how does their presence affect the home government's power to develop a basic needs strategy? A dominant role of multinationals in a developing economy, it appears, seriously circumscribes the planning power of the local government. In most countries where the multinationals have an important measure of control they become planners by default. Major social decisions about communications, consumption patterns, the growth of cities, transportation, and the like are made as byproducts of private profit maximizing strategies. That is true in the United States and other industrialized countries as well. The dependence of American society on automobiles and fossil fuels and the resulting concrete and asphalt landscape is the consequence of private commercial decisions which determined political choices. That is precisely how the market system is supposed to work.

But what happens when a government wishes to intervene by establishing planning decisions which modify the operations of the market. Any effort to redistribute income, goods, or services to the poor involves such decisions. A basic needs strategy involves shifting resources to people who are outside the market or are by the economic criteria of the society "unproductive." To invest in local health clinics, to build houses for people without money, to clean the water in rural areas where it is a necessity of life but not a commodity are contrary to the economic interests of multinational corporations. From the point of view of the corporation the priority public investments are roads, harbors, subsidies for high technology, and other expenditures to develop the infrastructure to support profitable private investment. Money should be spent on the productive enclaves of the society and not wasted on the rest. Spending money on those who do not produce, according to most economic theory, is a recipe for ruinous inflation.

The preferred strategy of the multinationals, investment to stimulate productivity (more capital per worker), runs directly counter to a basic needs strategy in every respect. Since an ever increasing proportion of the world population is unneeded in the global productive system, investments to stimulate productivity are irrelevant to them. As McNamara and the World Bank have discovered, the benefits of growth do not reach the poor. But the political power of multinational corporations is firmly committed against redistributive experiments as in Allende's Chile or in Manley's Jamaica. The power is now exercised principally through banks and international lending agencies. The huge debt owed by Third World countries to public and private banks provides effective leverage to discourage redistributive strategies that, from the viewpoint of the multinationals, threaten financial or political stability. The International Monetary Fund is demonstrating what Arthur Burns calls "a new assertiveness in monitoring the economic policies of its members" and is offering its "certificate of good standing," a condition of getting new loans or renegotiating old ones, only if the debtor countries practice the "responsible" economic policies that keep the poor hungry—freezing wages, cutting imports and private consumption, and eliminating social services and subsidies. Thus while conscientious development economists at the World Bank are wrestling with basic needs strategies, their colleagues across the street are setting conditions which make the satisfaction of basic human needs for the poor impossible.

The incompatibility between the global profit-maximizing strategies of the multinationals and national strategies to provide a floor for the whole population are not sufficiently perceived because officials are misled by the false analogies of European and North American development. The economist Michael Lipton has noted some of the crucial disparities between the development setting two hundred years ago in the now industrialized countries and in the Third World societies today. One point he makes is that the industrial elite in Europe and America had an incentive to integrate the poor into a national consumption community, to empower them to buy the products of the expanding factories. But that is not the goal of multinational strategies in Third World countries. The companies are creating through a transnational network a global market which integrates islands of affluence within many different poor countries. The market in any single country is extremely limited. The President of National Biscuit Company, for example, told me that the target in Brazil for a relatively cheap product such as Ritz crackers was 20 million (out of a population of 105 million). Thus mass production industry is not a force for great income equalization in the Third World as it was in Europe and North America.

There are many other major differences, of course, between the contemporary situation of the former colonial world and the pre "take-off" stage of the industrial nations. Britain at the beginning of the second decade of the last century, before the long process of increasing the economic and political power of the poor began, had only a third of its workers in agriculture. In most poor countries the figure is well over two-thirds. Only about 5% of the labor force is typically in the modern industrial sector. The elites are typically bureaucrats and traders rather than entrepreneurs, and when they are the latter, they are at least as likely to invest abroad as at home. All these factors help to explain why the stimulus of foreign investment and entrepreneurial energy from abroad is not creating the mass consumption societies that were the foundation of European and North American liberalism and the egalitarian trends of the last seventy-five years.

Perhaps the most crucial question of all in assessing the impact of the multinational corporation on poor countries concerns its role in the transformation of local politics and culture. Development is fundamentally a political process. A basic needs strategy based on the ethic of the zoo cannot succeed. There is not enough money in the world for a global welfare program, and such a program would not, as Denis Goulet points out, meet the basic human need for dignity and meaning.

Unless economic strategies can elicit a human response and help to mobilize the energies of the vast majority of people in the world, who happen to be poor, they will not substantially reduce inequalities or provide decent minimum levels of existence. A redistribution of economic benefits follows a redistribution of political power. People get their basic needs met when they are in a position to demand that they be met. The power to share in the rewards of society can come in many ways. It can come through armed struggle. It can come because of the rising value of labor power. It can come through revolutionary ideology. (The power of the Chinese peasant, to demand that his basic needs be met, comes not from the barrel of a gun but from his ability to use the rhetoric and ideals of the revolution to compel local bureaucrats and functionaries to do what the society expects of them.) A basic needs ideology is revolutionary because it requires changing political and economic relationships to make its realization possible.

The principal reason why multinational corporations play a reactionary role in the development process is that they have incentives to keep the existing political and economic relationships as they are or to change them in ways that promote their own stability. From the point of view of the corporation a poor country offers three possible attractions—raw materials, workers, and consumers. It is in its interest to have assured supplies at assured prices for as long as possible. Since governments have a key role in the decisions that determine price and availability, political stability, whatever the government (as long as it is cooperative) is a company objective. Governments that experiment with ending feudal relationships, shifting domestic power, or redistributing goods and services are by definition adversaries to be opposed. The widespread awareness throughout the Third World of the fate of Mossedegh, Arbenz, Allende, the leftist Peruvian generals, and many others inspires caution and cynicism among the Third World elite. The dependence upon multinationals restricts alternative policies for exploitation and use of raw materials. This is perhaps most obvious in the case of land. A commitment to export-led agriculture, typically dominated by foreign agri-business, means that land and resources to cultivate it, capital, fertilizer, machinery, etc., are not available to provide food for the people who live in the country.

Multinationals spread across Asia, Africa, and Latin America in the 1950s and 1960s in search of a cheap and docile labor force. The high wages paid to U.S. workers, which in the early postwar years bore no relationship to what Japanese or German factory owners paid their workers, forced U.S. companies to become multinational to preserve their competitive position. The impact on the U.S. labor movement and its power to bargain has been serious, and the resultant loss of jobs in key industries and regions has been devastating in economic and human terms. But, it is frequently argued, is not the transfer of jobs from the rich countries to the poor countries a progressive development that is leading to a world-wide redistribution of income? The reality, unfortunately, is that this process is helping to undermine the political preconditions for instituting basic needs strategies in both the developed and undeveloped societies. In the United States the loss of organized labor's bargaining power—the result of the mobility of capital— has meant a decline in real wages, a reversal of the favorable income distribution trends of the 1930s, and a declining interest on the part of the major unions in organizing the poor.

In the poor countries the development of "export platform" production centers has created a small "labor aristocracy," which frequently is paid better than workers in local plants and which develops class interests that are adverse to those of the peasant majority. If, as Michael Lipton persuasively argues, policies throughout the Third World (and everywhere else) are biased against agriculture, then the "labor aristocracy" has no interest in changing things. For several reasons this privileged group is likely to become ever more exclusive. (Privilege is a relative term, as anyone who has visited a Hong Kong sweatshop can attest.) As wages in the export platform countries rise, the companies are bringing in more of the labor-dispensing technology which they developed in the home country. Moreover, as the world economy continues to stagnate and transportation costs rise, multinationals are closing down marginal operations overseas. According to a study by Brent Wilson, an assistant professor of business at the University of Virginia, U.S. multinationals sold off 1359 overseas subsidiaries in the years 1971–75 or about 10% of all U.S. overseas subsidiaries. These tended to be in the labor-intensive low technology industries such as textiles, leather goods, and tires, precisely those that employ local labor. There is some evidence that companies are shifting marginal operations from one Third World country to another as wages rise in the established export platforms. A basic needs strategy must be based on stable employment. But basing an employment policy on the continued presence of multinationals is treacherous. The long-term political effect is division of the country and the discouragement of the political coalitions between workers and peasants needed to mobilize a society for change.

Perhaps it is the quest for consumers that has more impact on development than any other aspect of the multinationals' global strategy. We have already mentioned that the pool of potential consumers for the products of the most successful multinationals—automobiles, computers, transportation, household appliances, high technology for industry—is extremely limited. The wealthy and aspiring middle class who can afford these products are through consumption integrated into an international community and in the process detached from the national community. Put differently, the consumers of high technology and luxury goods are closer and feel closer to their counterparts in other countries who drink the same scotch, drive the same cars, wear the same clothes, eat the same food, and take the same vacations than they do to the destitute majority in their own country. Their future is tied to the prosperity of the companies in which they invest or for which they work. It is not tied to the general welfare of their country. Their interest is neither to extend democratic participation in their country, which they find threatening, nor to meet basic needs, which is a foreign and utopian idea, but to keep a lid on social discontents and to preserve their own mobility.

This is the real extent of the "brain drain" problem. The minority with the education, confidence, and the technical and political skills to change their own societies have no interest in doing so because their heart and their treasure are elsewhere. Thus they have every incentive to believe in economic fairy tales—to persuade themselves and others that the international economic relationships that have made them rich and given them the goods that give meaning to their lives will eventually enrich everyone else. The presence of the goods within the country has a powerful political effect that severely restricts the options of political leaders who wish to recast national priorities to meet basic needs. The disappearance of luxury goods from the stores as a result of Allende's decision to use scarce foreign exchange to meet basic human needs was a principal grievance of the Chilean middle class that mobilized them to support the overthrow of the regime.

What about the political impact of the transnationalization process on the poor majority? Does the appearance of goods and services that are beyond reach radicalize or immobilize people? Does the international consumer culture in the midst of squalor cause people to demand that their basic needs be met or is it a new opiate of the people which reinforces their passivity? The answers to these questions are not clear. We do know something of how consumption patterns of processed foods and soft drinks have changed diets and the way meager food budgets are spent, and the consequences, by and large, have been aggravated malnutrition. The baby-formula scandal in which multinational food company advertising persuades poor peasants to use prepared formula (to be mixed typically with contaminated water) instead of breast-feeding, which is free and safe, is evidence of the power of the marketplace ideology to persuade people to do things that are against their interest.

The most important political impacts, I believe, are more subtle. I know of no empirical studies on the point, but I have the feeling that the consumer values and consumer culture the multinationals bring with them destroy a principal source of psychological strength needed for effective political change: a sense of worth and dignity. The new cultural values assert that the purpose of a society is to produce and to consume in the international manner, but by that criterion a rapidly increasing proportion of the world population has no social role. Perhaps as many as two billion people on earth are not needed to produce and they have no money to consume. Why then are they here? Not for the same reasons their parents and grandparents lived because the family farm is gone, the village structure has completely changed, and so on. Even the traditional source of pride and badge of worth, producing a family, is now officially disparaged.

The political and economic system that operates in most of the world denies value to the majority of the world's population. This is the heart of the global human rights problem and it is the reason why the energy to mobilize societies to meet basic needs is lacking. There is no possibility of meeting basic human needs unless the energy of people themselves is released. That can happen only when the development process is guided by a set of values quite different from those which undergird the global shopping center.

Transnational Corporations and Basic Needs

Paul Streeten

The role of the transnational corporation (TNC) in development is already large and is of growing importance, and policies have to be evolved that enable governments to harness its potential for the benefit of the development effort. This paper starts with the premise that a fundamental objective of development is to meet the basic needs of the billion or so absolute poor people in the world, that some governments are prepared to commit themselves seriously to giving high priority to this objective, and that they wish to explore the role of TNCs in such an approach.

One of the attractions of the basic needs (BN) concept is that it provides a powerful organizing and integrating framework for a whole range of otherwise disparate and apparently intractable issues. One of these is the role of the TNC. When we ask ourselves what contribution can TNCs make to meeting the basic human needs of the absolute poor, the issues that are raised become, at least in principle, amenable to answers.

The basic needs approach consists of three components: adequate personal incomes, basic public services and participation. The contribution of the TNC clearly lies primarily in the area of the basic needs goods and services on which the personal incomes of the poor are spent, both producer and consumer goods, both final and intermediate products. It also covers the area in which the incomes of the poor may be earned, such as foreign trade, both in manufacturing and agriculture.

Appropriate Products

There has been a good deal of discussion of appropriate technology, and the charge has been raised that TNCs introduce excessively capital-intensive, and therefore inappropriate technologies into the developing countries. I shall return to this issue, but the first point to make is that the over-sophistication and over-specification lies more often in the *product* than in the *technology*. While the case for a "balanced diet" makes it impossible to substitute between very broadly defined product groups, such as food, clothing, household goods, transport, shelter, etc., the specifications of particular products within these broadly defined groups provide scope for choice. Food can be branded and advertised, packaged, highly processed and standardized to headquarter specifications, or it can be natural or semi-processed, variable in quality, locally grown, unpackaged. Transport can be by private cars, buses, motor bicycles, mopeds or bicycles. Shirts can be made with synthetic fiber, drip-dry, or with natural, locally grown fiber, washable, ironable. Agricultural machinery may be tractors or simple power tillers.

It is in the nature of the TNC that it possesses a monopolistic or oligopolistic advantage over its potential local rivals, for otherwise international investment would not occur. This oligopolistic advantage may take various forms, but one common form in consumer goods is the creation of goodwill through advertising and sophisticated marketing techniques, as in branded foods. Another form is the incorporation of Research and Development (R&D) expenditure, as in pharmaceuticals. A third form is large-scale production with the restriction on rival entry that this entails. These monopolistic advantages enable the firm to reap monopoly profits until the advantage is eroded by competition, when the firm has to renew its attempt to re-establish the advantage. The sophistication of the products, and the complexity of the technology determined by the products, are therefore not only a response to the high incomes and high savings in the mass markets of the developed countries, but they are of the very essence of the TNC. Very simple products cannot normally be protected through patents, trademarks, trade secrets or other forms of exclusion and are readily imitated. Even where they can be so protected, the appropriation of profits does not last long. Unless they are much cheaper to produce on a mass scale (as is the case with buses or mopeds), the TNC has no special advantage in producing them. It is for investigation why multinationals produce and sell simple basic needs products like bicycles, sewing machines, margarine, soap and washing powder, and whether small-scale domestic firms, if given access to capital, to other inputs, and to markets, might not be able to compete successfully. The presumption is that the TNC has no special advantage in supplying simple basic needs goods and services and that transformation in the direction of reduced dualism is likely to reduce the scope for its operations.

The provision of an adequate diet and health is an essential part of the basic needs approach. On present evidence, the branded, advertised and marketed food products and soft drinks of the TNCs do not appear to be capable of making a substantial contribution here. This is not the place to rehearse the scandals of some of the baby formula companies, or of some of the pharmaceutical firms, who have grossly overcharged for the active ingredients of drugs. In *The Nutrition Factor* (Brookings Institution, Washington, 1973, p. 158) Alan Berg concludes a careful survey of TNCs and nutrition by saying that, in spite of the substantial time and energy devoted by governments to involving big business, "there is little to show in the way of nutrition improvement. Nor are the prospects bright for reaching a significant portion of the needy with proprietary foods marketed in the conventional manner . . . the major impediment is the inability to reconcile the demand for corporate profit with a product low enough in cost to reach the needy in large numbers."[1]

Insofar as "appropriate" products of a simple, not over-specified kind, using local materials and local labor, have not been invented, so that there are gaps in the product range, there is clearly need for R&D. But for the reasons given, the TNC will not have the incentive to devote its R&D to this purpose. For, having spent possibly substantial sums on an innovation, rapid imitation will soon erode its profits and it will not be able to recoup its expenditure. It is the very fact that the social benefits on such innovations exceed the private, appropriable returns, and that markets in developing countries are more competitive, that leads to the minuscule research that is done on appropriate basic needs products. An example would be a cheap, say $50 refrigerator. The argument points to alternative methods of financing R&D.

Similar considerations apply to simple producer goods, like hand tools and power-driven equipment, both for small farmers and for small industrial and service enterprises. The appropriate technology may be missing or, though in existence, may be unknown in the country. But it is hard to see how the TNC could have an incentive to spend funds on developing such products. There might be more scope in supplying capital goods required as inputs into the public provision of basic services (road building equipment, equipment for geological surveys, medical equipment, drugs).

Technology

In spite of frequent charges that TNCs, compared with local firms, introduce excessively capital-intensive technologies into developing host countries, there is no evidence that *for the same product lines* TNCs use more inappropriate technology than local firms. Some evidence points to the opposite. The previous section argued that the real issue is not the technology for a given product, which is often dictated, at least within a range, by the specifications of the product, but the product choice itself. Thus, the technology employed in a steel plant is largely determined by the degree of sophistication of the final products for which the steel is needed.

There has also been controversy on the location of the R&D activities, developing countries complaining that parent countries monopolize the bulk of this activity. However, R&D is a high-skill-intensive activity and this type of skill is even scarcer than capital in developing countries. Only where research depends on local conditions (as in much agricultural research, on soil and climate) is there a strong case for the location of the research in the developing host country.

There is a clear need to devote substantially more R&D to the invention and dissemination of appropriate, capital-saving technologies and products, many of which have been identified. The difficulty, as already mentioned in the discussion of products, is that normally the TNC has no incentive to devote its resources to such research, because it does not offer the opportunity to recoup the full benefits derived from the expenditures, through monopoly pricing.

Nevertheless, there might still exist an unrealized potential of TNCs for transferring and adapting existing technology and for inventing new and appropriate technologies. In order to reap the maximum benefits, the developing countries would have to create the conditions for absorbing the contributions by the TNCs, possibly through joint ventures, conditions for training local counterparts, encouraging local research and fostering attitudes favorable to such absorption.

But, as far as simple, basic needs products, and simple, capital-saving technologies, adapted to local climatic and social conditions are concerned, there is no escape from the conclusion that it is in the nature of the TNC that it will not devote R&D funds to this purpose. The small, competitive local firms in the developing countries, on the other hand, do not have the market power and the means to embark on such research. The conclusion for policy again points to alternative ways of financing relevant R&D, either directly through government finance or indirectly through governmental compensation for innovators, the social benefits of whose inventions exceed their private ability to appropriate profits.

TNCs and Small-Scale Local Enterprise

It is controversial whether TNCs encourage or discourage local entrepreneurship in the "informal" sector (small scale artisans and service workers such as tailors, shopkeepers, transport workers, and so on). Some observers have adduced evidence on subcontracting, showing the stimulating impact of TNCs, others have produced evidence that local initiative has been stifled. The two positions are, of course, not inconsistent, for some types of activity might be encouraged, others discouraged. Government policies that have kept interest rates low and have rationed capital to large, including transnational firms and that have discriminated in government procurement in favor of these firms have reduced employment, increased inequality and run counter to a basic needs approach. The complexity of government regulations, the encouragement of collective bargaining, minimum wage legislation and similar measures also make it more difficult for small-scale domestic firms to compete with the TNCs.

The Contribution of TNCs

It is sometimes said that TNCs passively adapt to the economic and political environment that governments create. Like the corner grocer, the TNC is said to respond to ruling prices and caters for existing demand. Such a picture flies in the face of mounting evidence. TNCs have actively attempted to shape their environment, from attempting to overthrow a legally elected government (ITT in Chile), to bribing a president to reduce export taxes in order to break a banana cartel (United Brands in Honduras) to bribes to officials and royalty in order to sell aircraft (Lockheed, not a TNC, in a number of countries). Even if we rule out illegal, unethical and improper activities, it is clear that TNCs attempt to influence governments when negotiating about establishing their subsidiaries, about the terms of the contract, including such items as tariff protection, labor laws, tax provisions, etc.

If their role in shaping the economic and political environment has been systematically underestimated, their role in contributing capital has been overestimated. As much as three quarters of foreign investment by TNCs is now financed locally, either by retained earnings or through raising local capital. The special contribution of the TNC consists in the "package" of capital, technology, management and marketing. One of the problems in assessing the impact of the TNC on BN is that some components of the package may have desirable, others detrimental effects. The host country may not have the foreign marketing facilities that the

TNC provides, but the TNC's technology may aggravate local unemployment. Or the company may provide skills for production for domestic consumption, but the product may be suited only for the upper income groups. It is this fact, as well as more general cost considerations, that has led to the demand for "unbundling" the "package," and purchasing the missing components separately. But since the monopolistic strength of the TNC consists precisely in offering the whole "package" on a take-it-or-leave-it basis, it will be unwilling to agree to "unbundling."

TNCs and Employment

A BN approach calls for raising the productivity and earning power of the poor. One of the most important ways of doing this is to increase remunerative employment opportunities. Can the TNCs make a contribution to job creation? On past evidence, the answer is not encouraging. Estimates of overseas assets by TNCs in the Third World are unreliable but a plausible figure is that the stock of foreign capital in 1970 was $40 billion, of which half was located in Latin America and the Caribbean. This stock provided employment for approximately 2 million workers or roughly 3% of the labor force (United Nations, *Multinational Corporations in World Development*, 1973). The average capital cost of creating a job is therefore $20,000. It appears that, on past performance, TNCs cannot make a more than negligible contribution to employment creation.

A BN-oriented approach, by spreading purchasing power more widely, would, of course, reduce the incentives to produce sophisticated products requiring capital-intensive techniques. A turn to greater export-orientation would enlarge the scope for labor-intensive export industries, particularly for the location of labor-intensive processes or the production of labor-intensive components by vertically integrated firms in developing countries. But here again, technical innovation may shift the comparative advantage if, as seems likely, mechanization can replace these labor-intensive processes.

In spite of some opportunities, the specific advantages of TNCs in a BN approach would be considerably smaller. There would be less demand for sophisticated, mass produced consumer and producer goods. The scope for advertising and shaping tastes by sophisticated marketing techniques would be reduced. The profitability of R&D-intensive technology would fall. Both the need of host countries for TNCs and the incentive of these companies to operate in developing countries would decline.

Regional Integration

A BN approach, by attacking the prevailing dualism (in which a small privileged group has its links with the developed economies, while the rest remains in poverty), will tend to encourage intra-Third World trade. While at the moment the economies of the developing countries are largely competitive, there is considerable scope for complimentarity and expanding trade. There is a tendency for the poor to consume the simple products that they themselves produce, and for them to produce the products that they consume. There are clearly exceptions to this, and some basic needs goods and services might well be appropriately produced in a highly sophisticated and/or capital-intensive manner. But, as a rule, a BN approach will tend to encourage intra-Third World trade, investment and technical assistance.

Two distinct problems arise for the TNC. One is an anxiety shared by many countries. When several developing countries form a customs union, a free trade area or a region of closer co-operation, new profit opportunities arise for the already operating and for newly entering foreign companies. Policies have to be devised to insure a fair sharing of these profits between the customs union and the foreign companies.

The historical legacy of communications, transport, credit facilities and institutions will tend to reinforce the North-South connection, and the countries engaged in promoting collective self-reliance and regional cooperation may find it difficult to fit the TNCs into a pattern of South-South trade and investment.

Changes in infrastructure, reductions of trade barriers, etc., may help, but the historical and conventional North-South links may be hard to sever.

A second set of problems concerns the sharing of the gains from integration between different members of the customs union. The creation of a new form of international company, the shares of which would be held by the member countries of the customs union, might be one way of solving this problem, though it has so far not been successful. The proposal would be for the company to combine low-cost, efficient location and operation, not subject to political horse-trading, with sharing of the gains between member countries.

Alternatively, there can be agreement on other forms of compensation, such as arrangements to pay higher prices for the exports of the less industrialized member countries, or to permit their citizens to migrate within the region, or to locate universities and research institutes in the less developed partner countries.

Environment

In the new international division of labor which would be guided by differential pollution costs in different countries, the location of certain "dirty" processes in developing countries could be one of the functions of the transnational corporation, if the host countries are prepared to accept them. This could be done either by the firm locating "dirty" processes within its vertically integrated system of operations in a developing country where the social costs of pollution would be lower and the benefits from raising levels of living higher, or by transferring the whole operation to such a country. The argument would be analogous to that of locating unskilled or semi-skilled labor-intensive processes and products in developing countries. One important point to be investigated here is whether the TNC cannot be used as a pressure group to ensure access for these products to the markets of the developed countries, where protectionist pressures are disguised as a desire for environmental protection.

Bargaining

As the TNC has become one of the main vehicles of transferring modern, complex and changing technology from developed to developing countries, an important aspect of policy is the terms on which the technology is transferred. In settling the bargain and in drawing up the contract, a large number of items may be for negotiation. Some of these may refer to incentives such as protecting the market for the product or improving the attractiveness of inputs (public utilities, a disciplined labor force, absence of red tape); others may lay down conditions for sharing the benefits with the host country, such as tax provisions, the use of local materials, local participation in management, training workers, creating jobs, raising exports, etc.; others again will relate to policies such as conditions about repatriation of capital and profits, about raising local capital, etc. In this manner the consequences of the activities of the TNC can be tilted in the direction of meeting basic needs. Perhaps the most obvious instance is where the TNC itself makes no contribution to basic needs, but the tax revenue collected by the government is used for financing rural public works, which improve the position of the rural poor.

In order to achieve such gains, skilled and informed bargaining is necessary, Hitherto, multilateral technical assistance in negotiations of this type, and in training negotiators, has been on a very small scale. International organizations could render vital technical assistance in strengthening the bargaining power of developing countries in negotiating such contracts and contribute to an informed dialogue between managers of TNCs and public officials through training courses. What is needed is both direct technical assistance in drawing up contracts, possibly with the aid of a model contract, and formation, and encouragement of solidarity among developing countries, to avoid competitive concessions.

Institutions

Another important area of policy is the imaginative exploration of new legal and business institutions which combine the considerable merits of the transnational corporation with the maximum beneficial impact on basic needs satisfaction. This area comprises joint ventures, i.e., joint both between private and public capital and between domestic and foreign capital, which go further than window dressing by giving the developing host country access to information and decision making, and various provisions for divestment and gradual, agreed transfer of ownership and management from foreigners to the host country. Thus, countries wishing to curb the power of large groups in their manufacturing sector may find investment reduced. This may make it advisable to institute a "joint sector" in which public capital is combined with private national management with or without an equity stake, or public capital is combined with private international capital. Another possibility would be a management contract with a national or international investor.

Thought and action in this area have suffered from a poverty of the institutional imagination which has lagged behind the advance of the scientific and technological imagination. Discussions have turned partly on the ideological dispute between private and public enterprise. Yet, the real issues have little to do with ownership. Mixed companies can be devised that simultaneously harness private energy and initiative, yet are accountable to the public and carry out a social mandate, on the model of the British Commonwealth Development Corporation. Equally arid has been the dispute over the virtues and vices of private foreign investment. Here again, the task should be to identify the positive contributions of foreign firms and the social costs they impose on the host country, to see how the former can be maximized or the latter minimized, and to provide for gradual, agreed transfer to national or regional ownership and management. There is a need for a legal and institutional framework in which the BN objectives that are not part of the firm's objectives can be achieved, while giving the firm an opportunity to earn profits by contributing efficient management and technology.

Finally, a basic needs approach to development should explore the opportunities for a changed direction of the activities of TNCs. As we have seen, a basic needs approach would enlarge the scope for intra-Third World trade and investment. New types of

TNCs might emerge and should be encouraged. They might be smaller and more competitive. They might produce the simpler wage goods and services required by BN, employ more labor-intensive technologies, and draw more on local materials. They might make more use of local subcontracting, thereby encouraging local entrepreneurship and capital formation. TNCs have, in the past, shown great powers of adaptation. They have accepted increasingly host country conditions in the form of joint ventures, greater participation of local personnel and even minority share holdings. It might well be that their considerable flexibility will enable them to define a place for themselves in a BN approach to development.

Impact of Trade and Debt
on the Developing Countries

Philip Land, S.J.

At every point of world economy today interdependence—
growing interdependence—is the stark reality. The impact of trade
and debt on the developing countries[1] is another undeniable instance of this. For both trade and debt are two-way streets between
North and South with intra-North and intra-South complications.
The North finds in the developing nations an indispensable market.
The South equally needs the industrial world as a market for its
products. To purchase the equipment for its economic development the South is prepared to go into debt with the North. With the
quadrupling of oil prices in 1974 the non-oil producing among the
developing nations have huge and mounting deficits as the oil-
producing of the Third World nations build vast reserves or earnings.

What, of course, makes this interdependence frightful for the
Third World is that a sneeze in the North can spell a flu epidemic in
the South. When the USA and its associates are working their way
through the old familiar recessions or today's combinations of
stagnation with inflation, troubles mount for the poor South. The
North reduces its buying of the South's exports. The South which
over recent decades has been building up its indebtedness as it
buys the North's industrial equipment for development finds it
can't pay off its debts from export earnings.

In fact, it is pushed into further indebtedness, for developing
nations are understandably unwilling to shelve development plans
awaiting a better buying mood in the North. Further, as its debts
and servicing charges on them mount the South discovers that their
Northern bankers, private and such multi-governmental "banks"

as the International Monetary Fund, begin to pressure them to balance their budgets by reducing imports. This means cutting into needed welfare. In short, the poor become poorer. Later we shall see that this austerity program is a subject of deep controversy.

But, it is not only the South that tightens its belt. As the South reduces imports the North automatically must cut back on exports to the Third World with serious impact on employment.

It is this staggering—and chronic—problem that is with us and growing if we must look forward to ever-recurring recessions in the North with weak revivals.

I
FIVE AVENUES FOR GRAPPLING WITH THE PROBLEM

Five avenues for grappling with the problem gain attention. First, the developing nations could seek a development with none or minimal reliance on debt. Second, the North could help by increasing aid on concessional terms for development. Third is the road of increased earnings from raw materials through increased exports, better prices, processing, etc. Fourth would be cancellation of some debts and re-scheduling of others on longer terms with longer grace periods. Fifth would be some bold imaginative scheme such as a Marshall Plan for the Third World.

One approach to this is the famous link that figured so centrally in the debates of UNCTAD III in Santiago, Chile, 1972. The basic idea there was to use SDRs of the International Monetary Fund. These Special Drawing Rights, a costless banking operation in the view of proponents of the link, are designed to increase liquidity in the world for trade and other transactions. The idea would be to put these first to the credit of the developing nations. As they drew upon them for purchases they would be cycled into the world spending system. It was an insightful British economist who at that conference urged its acceptance upon the delegates precisely as being a form of the Marshall Plan. As the Marshall Plan, while building up Europe also created jobs for the USA, so the Link[2] could build up the Third World while at the same time increasing employment in the North.

But the scope of our paper is not to explore these five avenues. It is more limited—trade and debt impact. Yet we cannot escape some discussion of the five for they weave their way into the complexity of our subject.

In between concessional aid and a Marshall Plan and sharing with both the character of transfers of wealth from the North to the South are the much-discussed approaches to automatic taxation of the North for development. Any number of schemes have been discussed: a tax on undesirable rich world consumption, pollution, arms spending. Exploitation of the ocean depths is another candidate. What is particularly sought is automaticity so that the poor South can rely on an assured fund. A $10 to $12 billion annual transfer with 90% grant component is often mentioned. Thus they would not need to cut off development purchases when export earnings fail.

From the days of Mahatma Ghandi many have pleaded for the kind of development that avoids external debt. Obviously, if developing countries were to choose to limit their material development they could avoid excessive reliance on foreign resources. One active promulgator of the desirability and concrete possibility of such development was the late E. F. Schumacher, author of *Small Is Beautiful*. Once people were to decide on relying on themselves and their own resources they would discover that a simpler and less expensive technology. Fuel requirements would fall off. There would be less reliance on high-technology machinery.

This road of self-reliance suggests a further consideration about development. Exports of a country's raw materials for today's earning purposes may come to be seen as a disastrous choice since those very materials become necessary to meet the future needs of a country's own expanding population.

This article is not the place to pursue the theme of aid, but the following picture ought to show how weak a reed it has become for the poor world to have to rely on.

The total of Official Development Assistance, on concessional terms, of the NATO nations that constitute the OECD

(Organization for Economic Cooperation and Development) has been essentially static over the past ten years despite the fact that real income of the OECD nations rose by 40% in the same period. The result is that as a percentage of GNP (gross national product) ODA has fallen from .42 in 1966 to .33 of 1% in 1976. That is exactly half of the target proposed by the UN General Assembly in 1970.[3] And while some of the OPEC group give about 2% of their GNP on concessional terms—mainly to a few Arab, Muslim countries— this does not remotely meet the gravity of the situation in the oil-importing developing countries which results from the six-fold hike in oil prices.

II
ROLE OF TRADE IN DEVELOPMENT

This is our third avenue toward solving our interdependent problems. Half of the remainder of this paper will be devoted to it. Then we shall explore the fourth avenue, that of debt relief. The fifth, for the reason already given, will be omitted.

Developing world trade divides into export of raw materials, processed goods and manufacturers. In the first division raw materials include agricultural commodities such as foods, tropical beverages like coffee and tea, sugar, meat and vegetable oils, and raw materials of industry like cotton and rubber. In addition, commodities embrace metals—manganese, tin, copper, and, of course, petroleum and natural gas. The existence of vast deposits of manganese in the ocean depths opens up vast new possibilities. In addition to commodities, the developing nations hope and intend to become the processors of an increasing percentage of these same commodities. They also want—and some are already on the road—to becoming important exporters of manufactured goods.

Commodity export still accounts for 50% of the export income of the non-oil producing among the developing countries. Six of those, now termed the middle-income among the developing countries, including such countries as Brazil, Mexico, Taiwan, rely much more on export of manufactured goods.

What Processing Can Mean

Processing of commodities includes all the stages between their raw material and their final consumption form. It may be divided into semi-processing and processing. Before raw cocoa beans become a chocolate bar there must intervene the stages of grinding and refining. At these stages obviously a lot of value is added to the raw product. Presently most of this value accrues to the rich nations. This they achieve by the simple devise of hiking the duty on imports from zero for raw coffee beans (since they need them), to high duties on processed coffee, and still higher on coffee ready for marketing. The annual bill paid by consumers in the industrial North for beverages, food and manufactured goods originating in the raw materials produced by the developing world amounts to over $200 billion. Of this sum the producers of the raw materials get only $30 billion. Just as within a nation the farmer gets relatively little of the consumer's dollar, with most of it going to processors and distributors, so too in the case of the developing countries. The value added to the product of their fields goes in part to their own middlemen. But largely it goes to those who control most of the processing, finishing and distributing of these raw materials, even within the developing countries themselves. And these are the processors of the rich world. If more of the processing could be shifted to the Third World it could gain as much as $150 billion in annual earnings. Contrast that with OECD's meager $8 billion in aid.

Role of Manufactures-Export

Presently the developing world produces only about 7% of the world's total of industrial goods and manufactures. One of the planks of the Fourth UNCTAD, held in Nairobi in May 1976, was to increase that percentage to 25% by the year 1985.

Part of that effort looks to import-substitution. By that is meant an effort to become less dependent on the industrial West by creating indigenous industries to meet local needs. Space permitting one would pause here to discuss the conditions under which import-substitution is economically feasible. The main problem is that of finding a market large enough to permit reducing unit costs of production. The more the developing nations can work out regional cooperation the more they will be able to achieve import-substitution.

The other direction of such industrialization is export, which we explained above. It is the belief of the president of the World Bank[4] that the developing nations could increase the volume of their commodity exports by about 50% by 1985 and that of manufactured exports could be tripled, increasing the latter from 1975's $33 billion to about $94 billion by 1985.

Trade Liberalization

If controlling more of the gains from agricultural production through retaining their processing is an important, perhaps the most important way to improve trade earnings, freer entry into rich markets is another.

Recently, Third World trade interest has concentrated on achieving remunerative and stable prices for the commodities they export and debt relief. The result has been to put onto a backburner trade liberalization which had hitherto been of primary concern. We do not explore here the reasons for this. But we must note in passing two things. First, that a 1970–71 World Bank study demonstrates a weak correlation existing between export stability and growth of GNP but a strong correlation between growth of export earnings and growth in GNP. Trade entry apparently has bigger payoff than stabilization. If overall exports are up, instability is not all that much of an obstacle to growth. In addition, according to McNamara in his Presidential Address of 1977, if the OECD countries were to dismantle completely continuing barriers to entry of manufactured goods from the Third World, the latter could by 1985 earn still another $24 billion beyond the tripling of revenues from export of manufactures projected for 1985.[5]

The continued removal of barriers to goods from the Third World was a prominent plank in the UN's Strategy for the Second

Development Decade. Back in 1970 they called for agreement not to raise tariff and non-tariff barriers but to reduce these. Recognizing that freer entry would mean job displacement in the receiving countries, the UN strategy called for effort by governments to assist the adaptation and adjustment process and to help affected workers find alternative employment.

UNCTAD's Integrated Commodity Program

To freer entry for the South's products and retention of more of the value through processing, we must now add the avenue of higher export prices and protection of export earnings through price stabilization. There is also a form of temporary earnings stabilization. This is compensation payments for periods when due to an unexpected drop in supplies earnings fall off. But all of this can best be discussed within the framework of the program of UNCTAD.

All these topics have long been before the world community. At least as early as the 1930's an attempt was made to negotiate a wheat agreement. Sugar agreements go back to that period also. After World War II new efforts were mounted and coffee, cocoa and tin were included. These agreements have had a chequered career in various forums—GATT, FAO, UNCTAD from the mid-sixties, and still other forums created by consortia of interested countries.

It was frustration over failure of these, including those under its own auspices, that induced the Secretariat of UNCTAD to shift strategy in the preparation of its Fourth International Conference held in Nairobi in May 1976. Negotiators on the part of the consuming nations as well as commodity-producers shared frustration because the interests between these two blocs were so divergent. But within the consuming nations there were divergences between consumers of final products and processors and distributors. Speculators who might or might not be also processors and distributors had interests of their own. On one point the North was adamant in telling Southern producers not to try to use negotiations to lift prices above their long-run equilibrium, and not to expect the North to help finance the required buffer stocks. That was the South's own problem!

The producers were themselves divided. For example, before World War II, virtually all coffee producers were in Latin America. After the war several countries of Africa became strong producers. Among all such producers there are struggles over market-sharing. Still others produce materials for which long-term demand is not brisk. These need a program of diversification rather than price negotiations. Others of the Group of 77 have become important exporters of manufactured goods. These are more interested in freer access to capital markets together with debt relief.

From this welter of conflicting interests and approaches—to which could be added the innate difficulties of deciding on the range of an allowable price variation and how to stockpile the commodity and finance the latter, UNCTAD people came to realize that only an *integrated approach* could salvage their commodities program. Over the months before Nairobi an abundance of literature poured out from Geneva. Meanwhile the Group of 77 met twice at the ministerial level to iron out divergences among themselves in order to present a solid front at UNCTAD IV.

What, then, was the integrated program? Commodity market management is certainly the central piece. This was to embrace a remunerative level of prices and stabilization for eighteen commodities, to be accompanied in the case of at least eight by the creation of buffer stocks. These latter were to be financed from a Common Fund though the buffers would be administered by separate bodies for each of the commodities involved.

But even such stabilized prices do not guarantee a level of *income*. That depends also on quantities exported. The latter can be affected from both the demand side and the supply side. Sudden changes in either can result in deficits in export earnings in the short-run. Such deficits have been met by compensation payments. UNCTAD asked that these be increased.

The program also took note of the great gains to be achieved by increasing the amount of processing of commodities effected within the Third World. Finally, in view of the fact that long-term prospects are not good for some raw materials, the program called for financing of diversification, possibly from the Common Fund.

UNCTAD's Common Fund

The Common Fund is so integral to UNCTAD's Integral Commodities Program that it is frequently taken to stand for the whole ICP. In fact, it is only one aspect of the whole—the financial side of it. The CF is not intended to be operative in commodity markets. Each of the individual commodities would have its own managing organization. The task of these, after an agreement had been negotiated, would be to maintain the price within the negotiated limits. This it would do mainly by building up buffer stocks when prices for the individual commodities were favorable, that is, when the price for the commodity tended to sag, and by selling off stocks into the market when the price tended to rise above the established ceiling.

The CF would lend to these "owners" of the individual stocks so that they could buy stocks. The CF would be repaid by the commodity organizations as the latter received payment upon selling off stocks.[6]

The case for a CF is argued by UNCTAD's secretariat as follows. Most fundamentally, the fund is an instrument permitting the Third World to have a greater voice in commodity markets to offset the power of big buyers. Second, the CF should prove a catalyst for the negotiation of the individual agreements. The idea here is that since poor countries do not possess by themselves adequate funding for stocks, these are a weak reed to lean upon for financing. But in a cooperative effort they could make their proportionate financial contribution, especially since operation of their commodity stocks would permit payment of interest charges.

UNCTAD also believes that the CF would prove much more economical than separate funding of each of the ten commodities. It would be able to get better terms on its borrowing because of the quantity. It would pool risks, again adding to its bargaining strength in the capital market. Reduction in risks and pooled financing requirements would stem from the fact that normally not all commodity prices are moving in the same direction, so there are offsets.

Compensatory Financing

As seen, compensatory financing also figures in an important way in the ICP by covering temporary declines in export earnings. If we look to our own domestic agricultural programs we can better grasp its role. The domestic equivalent of price agreements is an agreement between government and farmers to stabilize their prices through price supports. But this does not meet one other problem. Suppose the market is so weak in demand that the salable volume will add up to poor earnings even with supported prices. To meet this problem the US government provides deficiency payments. These are a form of compensation. Compensatory financing therefore is lending to shore up producers when export earnings are temporarily soft. This stabilization of earnings ought to be seen, not as a substitute for price stabilization but as a complement.

UNCTAD IV, Nairobi

The story of the frustration experienced at Nairobi has been told many times and we need not repeat it. What did emerge as holding possibilities for the future was this program agreed to by the OECD as well as the Group of 77, though with reservations.

1. Preparatory discussions should take place for the eighteen commodities of interest, with this operation to be concluded by February 1978.

2. A Common Fund should be negotiated by March 1977.

3. Final negotiation conferences on the eighteen commodities were to be carried out through 1978.

III
CURRENT U.S. OFFICIAL POLICY ON TRADE

In the sections ahead we shall look at US policy with respect to seven aspects of the Integrated Commodity Program. We shall find that the United States is relatively open in principle to trade liberalization. It now positively favors price stabilization through commodity agreements but opposes any lifting of commodity prices above their "equilibrium." The US especially opposes this if effected through producers' associations or indexation. It has come round to the Common Fund support in principle, as an adjunct to price stabilization. It has always supported compensatory financing. Let us look at these and then evaluate their impact upon the developing world.

U.S. Policy on Trade Liberalization

Unfortunately, there seem to be only small prospects of further trade liberalization at the moment. The North continues to pour some $20 billion into protecting its farmers from the South's agricultural products. It gives protection equally to its industrial workers and investors. And in the US a recent report by the Charles Kettering Foundation of Dayton demonstrates that, with high unemployment, protectionist sentiment runs very high. An astonishing 85% of people interviewed said that keeping out foreign products to save domestic jobs ranks as a very important public policy goal.

All present indications are that the US government, while affirming more trade liberalization in principle, is prepared to respond selectively to the threat of job losses from imports; though it would only be fair to the Administration to acknowledge that they have dampened down hopes for any widespread curtailing of imports. However, until the government is prepared to make serious and sustained efforts to help workers and communities find alternative employment it is hard to see how the people directly affected can be exhorted to submit to unemployment.

Two further considerations deserve attention. The first is that most of the jobs lost are owing to imports from other developed countries like Japan and not to imports from the poor nations. There is room for discrimination here. Second, the Third World is a very important market for exports from the industrial North. Unless we are prepared to pay for those exports ourselves through a Marshall Plan type of aid, the poor world can pay for them only by its corresponding exports.

U.S. Policy on "Remunerative" Prices

There can be nothing more explicit than the rejection by Julius Katz, Assistant Secretary for Economic and Business Affairs of the Department of State, of any attempt to lift prices of raw materials above their "long-term, equilibrium trend." He states ". . . we do not view commodity agreements as an instrument to increase resource transfers to developing countries by fixing prices above their equilibrium levels."[7]

No less explicit is Fred Bergsten, Assistant Secretary for International Affairs, Department of the Treasury. "We reject," he says, "any thought of agreements that would raise prices above their market levels."[8]

The South's call for more remunerative prices for their raw materials must, nevertheless, strike a cord of sympathy for anyone who believes in a just wage. According to that theory anyone bearing responsibility for a family has the right to an income that makes it possible for him and his family to live in decency according to standards of the country where he resides. This principle is honored in the United States in the minimum wage along with unemployment compensation and deferred old-age security and other welfare payments. It is equally at the heart of parity prices which seek to bring the farmers' income up to that of industrial workers.

Why, one is forced to ask, should not a just wage be applicable to workers of other parts of the world in recompensation for the products they bring to our tables and homes? Why should not a Colombian coffee worker get from American consumers a price that makes it possible for him to raise his family in decency?[9]

However persuasive this logic it does not appeal to consumers who cannot bring themselves to regard Third World commodity workers in the same way that they regard American farmers. American policy-makers for their part allege that such additional remuneration lifts prices above their long-term normal equilibrium level. It is an apparently inexorcisable myth that we enjoy freely competitive markets in commodities. But surely experience bears out that markets for minerals and most commodities are in the hands of the few, and, therefore, are oligopolies. The few may be government buyers. More often they are multinational businesses which both produce and market. Other important actors may be speculators in commodities. It does not seem reasonable to argue that commodity agreements are more likely to cause misallocation of resource use than the interventions of the few powerful dealers.

It should be added that the essential question is what factors ought to enter into the determination of long-term eqilibrium. One can readily acknowledge the existence of such factors from experience. But should not the principle be that the price of a product must permit a minimum wage floor? The consensus in America is after all that goods cannot be produced or sold under conditions that preclude a minimum wage. Why cannot that American consensus be extended in support of products we buy from the Third World?

U.S. Opposes Pricing By Producers' Association

Out of frustration at their inability to get important OECD nations to support "social pricing," developing nations have sought more and more to imitate the success of OPEC. Why cannot the producers of bauxite, the exporters of copper, the growers of coffee band together to hike their prices? Why not, indeed? In fact producers' associations have been created since 1974 for copper and bauxite. Recession in the industrial world has not favored their efforts to improve prices. Copper prices have fallen off disastrously.

What, of course, is essential to the success of any such cartel is a lack of alternatives for the importing customers. This is the situation with OPEC. It is not so to the same degree for industrial materials and minerals. Stockpiles of copper, etc., are depleted during a recession rather than additional stock bought while waiting for lower prices to resume buying. Huge deposits of copper and bauxite are found in rich countries. This reduces the unity among producers. Finally, metals can either be substituted for or used more economically. For example, the amount of tin in tin cans is steadily reduced. And materials other than copper have proved efficient electric conductors.[10]

U.S. Opposes Indexation

The idea behind indexation is to tie prices of significant Third World commodities to some measure of prices for industrial goods, so that as the latter moves up commodity prices will also advance proportionately. UNCTAD's secretariat has developed a considerable body of literature on the topic. There is serious question whether the link of commodity prices to industrial prices would allow for a proper shift in relationships among these various prices on one side and the other when long-term demand for the specific commodities would change. Equally, productivity improves at different rates and would receive no proper registration in a general indexing. At the moment, indexation is not prominently before the world community and we may, therefore, set it on a backburner for the time being.

U.S. Favors Stabilization

The more conservative voices within the Administration which tend to regard any administration of price as against the free market appear to have lost out to those who are now committed to stabilization. But these latter are quite frank about it. They have suddenly discovered that American interests can be served by such stabilization. The official statements push the gain for national self-interest almost to the exclusion of any suggestion that stabilization is welcomed also by the developing countries—

which is, in fact, the official position. The playing-down of the latter is dictated by what the Administration construes as exclusive preoccupation on the part of the public with its own worries. Public opinion testing on these questions seems to depend very much on what question is asked and when. But this is not a topic to enter upon here.

The first national interest to be served by commodity agreements is the assurance of supplies. It was this that principally motivated Henry Kissinger, Secretary of State at the time of UNCTAD IV, to propose, in virtual opposition to the Group of 77's agenda of the Integrated Commodity Program, his International Resources Bank. Much of the Third World saw the bank as a gimmick serving exclusively the interest of the rich nations. They were suspicious too that the investment funds would flow mostly through the hands of First World multinational corporations interested in funding for mining operations. Administration officials now believe that if they enter into negotiations on price stabilization this will provide them a viable alternative to the Kissinger Bank and give them the right to see to it that supplies are not unduly kept off the market, and that adequate investment for exploitation of new sources of supply is assured.

The second way in which commodity stabilization is now seen to serve US interests is their contribution to the fight against inflation. Once again we turn to the testimony of Katz:

We know from recent US experience that in periods of tight supply, rising commodity prices transmit inflationary impulses throughout the economy. Through their effect on the cost of living index, they push up the wage-price spiral. The rise in costs become embedded in the economic structure and persists long after the commodity markets have turned round.[11]

Bergsten supports this, giving a somewhat different accounting of the inflationary pressure generated:

Producers of manufactured goods and food processors often justify additional increases in their prices on the basis of cost increases stemming from rising prices for their raw materials. However, these increases are not likely to be withdrawn when raw material prices recede. The effect is a ratcheting up of the general consumer price index which in turn provides justification for higher wage increases.[12]

U.S. Not Responsible for Failure in Negotiations

Once again we may return to the two eminent spokespersons of the Administration in their testimony on Capitol Hill. Julius Katz maintains that in every case up to the present where the US failed to pursue negotiations it was that technical considerations made plain that the agreement was either unfair or unviable. On the US's failure to enter the recent cocoa agreement he argues that the agreement is cumbersome and potentially disruptive of the market and combines features of export quotas and buffer stocks, and finally that the pricing formula is inflexible.[13]

He was supported in this by Bergsten. More than Katz he stressed that negotiation processes are long and complex. He adds that "there are not too many commodities where effective agreements are likely to prove feasible."[14]

U.S. Endorses the Common Fund

One of the meager gains from the ill-starred CIEC meetings was that the American negotiators at the end supported the Common Fund. Uncertainty as to how significant in fact that support would be may have been dissipated, again, in the testimony of Katz and Bergsten.

Katz's affirmation takes the form of stating the administration's support of a fund that would facilitate the financing of buffers provided such were financially viable and acceptable to the broad range of countries represented at UNCTAD.[15] Bergsten supported the Common Fund as being "a pooling of economies on the financial side. . . ."[16]

However encouraging for the Group of 77 this testimony of

mid-June might have seemed, the fact is that in November's crucial negotiations in Geneva the 77 felt constrained to pull out because they could see no sign that the US and the OECD in general were prepared for serious negotiation beyond principles.

U.S. View of Compensatory Financing

While still Secretary of State, Kissinger, speaking at the Seventh Special Session of the UN, called for a strengthening of the IMF's Compensatory Financing Facility, established in 1963. We have already seen the purpose of this fund. That fund disbursed from 1963 to 1975 about $1.2 billion to developing countries in trouble with their export earnings. In 1975, terms of the facility were further liberalized with US approval. In effect this permits developing world members of the IMF to draw up to 75% of their holdings of Special Drawing Rights and to draw, not as before just 25% in one year, but 50%.

Other facilities have been created within the Fund lately. But these refer more generally to Third World development assistance and may therefore be treated in our next section on debt.

Discussion on trade in this paper is limited to the agenda of ongoing UNCTAD negotiations. Other important considerations are thus omitted. The GATT negotiations, for instance, being conducted in the same city of Geneva are of potentially great importance for the Third World. Also the recently agreed IMF acceptance of flexible exchange rates, provides a tool of protection at least as significant as tariff barriers. Then there are non-tariff barriers—restrictive business practices—which are being probed by the UN's Committee on a Code of Conduct for Transnational Corporations.

Finally there are structural changes in trade. Import substitution of manufactured goods by Third World countries has not been slowed down by economists' criticisms. And in the same field of manufactured goods there is the surprisingly sharp advance made in the Third World's share of this.

This latter phenomenon must be linked to the growth of intra-firm trade in manufactured goods on the part of multinational corporations, whether this be through majority ownership, minority ownership, lending or licensing of technology, know-how, etc. (One understands why some developing countries are prepared to have their products marketed in the developed countries through the multinationals' brand names and marketing outlets.) What intra-firm trading is doing is of course to decrease what little arms-length negotiation ever existed (there has long been a remarkable degree of market concentration through price fixing, allocation of markets, agreed bidding, etc.), and to increase centrally planned decisions on volume and price. The Third World to defend its products must move toward (1) more intra Third World cooperation in production, marketing, financing; (2) the creation of multinationals of its own—or buying into existing multinationals; (3) moving more aggressively on already existing large-scale marketing such as national boards.

IV
THE DEBT PROBLEMS OF THE THIRD WORLD

Let's first set up the problem. Under present financial arrangements debt and trade appear starkly in reciprocal relation. But where a few years back trade dominated the relation, debt since 1973 has taken over this role. The non-oil producing of the developing nations must get outside financing to pay for their skyrocketed oil imports, as well as food, fertilizer and industrial goods. They can attract such capital only if they are viewed as credit-worthy by banks and other private sources of financing. Their credit-worthiness depends upon exporting more than they import, that is avoiding too many deficits on their current accounts.

Payments for oil by the industrial countries complicates the Third World's trade/debt problem. For the four and then six-fold increase from 1972 on is a partial cause of the industrial world's present recession. That means reduced buying from the developing countries at the very moment that these latter desire to export more. With the recession of 1974, the non-oil producing countries of the Third World began to understand that OPEC must be counted among the enemy.

A shifting in terms of trade between North and South would help. But that hinges on expansion in the North, and this in turn on oil prices. The trade/debt problem would of course be lightened if OPEC were to take back in exports from the non-oil producing countries of the Third World what the latter pay out for oil imports. But OPEC has very little demand presently for minerals and raw materials while it prefers industrial goods from the North to those manufactured in the South.

In this bind what can the countries we are concerned with do? Go protectionist, e.g., by import-substitutes? Despair? Fight?

The Debt Situation

Recent OECD studies show that all developing countries by 1977 held over $200 billions of debt. Of these the non-oil producers held $172. UNCTAD now believes that by the end of 1978 the debt will be $253 billions. We have already seen that the debt began to mount astronomically after the hikes in oil, which accounts for at least 50% of total debt. The remainder is explained by staggering increases in the cost of food, fertilizers and industrial goods.

The total outstanding debt of middle-income countries was $112.5 and will be $211.5 billions in 1980. Extrapolating it will by 1985 amount to $410. Similar extrapolation for the poorest countries sees their debt rise from $47.5 in 1980 to $86.3 in 1985.[17]

A few comments about this debt. First, governments, not private sources, have taken care of the debt needs of the poorest. On the contrary, the middle-income countries rely very much on private financing. For the period of 1973–76 alone private credits to these countries rose by $35 billion.

A second remark is that while the debt measured by interest relative to export earnings is burdensome: 14% for some, 20% for others and Mexico and Brazil running at 40%, the burden is drastically reduced in terms of inflation. Thus deflating the debt by the borrowing country's export price index, debt rises slowly, barely 8% over 1972.[18] And while 1980 debt total for all non-oil developing countries will be $259 billion, stated in 1976 dollars that reduces to $193. But deflated or not, the debt is huge and fast growing. Moreover, its growth from 1973 has been in great measure owing to factors outside the control of the debtors: jacked up prices of oil, fertilizers and food, recession among the industrial states, general inflation on the North side of the world.

It is this situation that prompts the secretary of UNCTAD to suggest that we need a new definition of debt troubles. Presently it is defined as that moment in which a country is likely to default. Mr. Gamani Correa suggests that it should be that moment in which debt servicing seriously impinges on a country's ability to import what is needed for development. By that standard all the low-income countries (29) plus those most seriously affected (16) are in debt trouble.

To what extent the middle-income countries are also—on this definition—in debt trouble is harder to say. During 1976 ten of them managed to reduce their total current deficit by more than a third. This was partly owing to better prices for commodities at the moment, and partly to restraint on imports. But Zaire had to have its debt rescheduled, while Peru, Turkey (and Portugal) are being accommodated. But if there was improved debt performance, will that, in the first place, continue to be possible as debts rise astronomically; and second at what cost of slowing down of development plans? For this latter, we saw how important is the Third World's ability to sell on world markets and how much that is conditioned by expansion in the North. Can the South rely on this?

So there are optimists and pessimists on Third World debt. On the very optimistic side are the International Monetary Fund (IMF) in its 1977 year-end report as also the World Bank in its similar report. The optimists rely on the fact of no default, on prompt payment by the ten countries which account for three-quarters of all debt owed to private sources by non-oil developing countries. They are also confident that private sources can continue to be relied upon.

Is the UNCTAD Forum Meeting the Need?

Before stating the case of the doubters, let us look at what progress has been made on debt at UNCTAD since its Fourth

Conference held in Nairobi, May 1975. UNCTAD's secretariat reports a breakthrough at its March 11, 1978 meeting. The US State Department was subsequently reported as perceiving a good North/South balance and that the Group of 77 had shown themselves more flexible, thus permitting concrete proposals.

What in fact did the Group of 77 get? Two things. First "retrospective terms adjustment," on public loans but on a case-by-case basis. Equivalently, this means that public holders of debt (governments) will reduce charges on past debt to present concessional terms. This will in effect mean (given OECD's intention to increase the grant amount in loans) converting the past debt of the poorest countries into grants.

Prior to the March meeting four countries had already announced intention to convert debt for the poorest into grants: Sweden, Switzerland, Canada and Australia. At the meeting several joined these in announcing a like intention: Great Britain, West Germany, Denmark (Australia and Norway were already giving only grants in aid to the poorest). Four others—France, Belgium, Japan and the USA—all require legislative authority for such measures.

President Carter, according to one report, is prepared to endorse that proposal of the Humphrey Bill for reorganization of aid which proposes conversion of US loans into grants for the neediest nations. Interest on $520 million would be forgiven and the principal be converted from dollars into local currencies for development.[19] But the US will insist on country-by-country debt forgiveness. In partial justification administration spokespersons point out that Uganda is among the debtors.

What did UNCTAD offer the middle-income countries at the same March meeting? The proposal was made to have a group of experts prepare a report on the problem of the middle-income countries for the May meeting of UNCTAD. Apparently the Group of 77 did not press, as they did at Nairobi in May 1976, across-the-board rescheduling of debt of middle-income countries—a proposal then opposed even by several middle-income countries—because it would destroy their credit-worthiness with private lenders.

Why the Pessimism?

Pessimism about the non-oil producing countries of the Third World continuing to receive adequate financing of their debt turns on two interrelated factors. The first is the global environment they will confront. Will it be one of strong enough expansion on the part of industrial countries to ease competition from the developing world? Or will it be one of repeated recessions carrying in their wake the protectionist temptation? The pessimists believe there is all too much likelihood of failure of industrial expansion and consequent protectionism.

The other related factor is private financing. Take the banks. Will they continue[20] to lend in proportion to needs? Widespread belief is that they will not. Why not? The answer is that banks are profit-making institutions.[21] On the one hand this justifies their refusal to treat loans on a let-bygones-be-bygone basis. It also explains why they are nervous over default since it would take very large loans in subsequent years to make up for the profit lost on default. One can also understand their legitimate indignation when Peru recently, instead of paying back loans to OECD banks, turned over $200 million of OECD money to pay for the import of arms from the USSR.

So profit-making has its reasonable side. On the other hand, the profit motive may induce banks to curtail their lending to the Third World on various grounds. One would be such an expansion in the industrial North that there would be strong demand for loans for capital investment. A second would be the banks' re-evaluation of the riskiness of some Third World lending. In this they are being abetted by US bank controllers who do believe that many banks are over-extended and must make both quantitative and qualitative changes. If, then, the banks do reduce their Third World lending, what institution remains to take care of the unmet needs of Third World financing?

The IMP as Last Resort

We have seen that bilateral governmental aid will, hopefully, meet the debt of the poorest countries. But what institution will match the global needs of the Third World? One could imagine various solutions. Most, however, turn on the IMF—and much more than just the Witteveen facility—as the proper institution to meet the need. But this raises grave questions about the conditionality imposed by the Fund. It also raises such new questions for American foreign policy as the following. Should the Fund lend to national security states—there are some eighty—which abuse civil and political rights?[22] Should the Fund refuse loans to countries which show no concern for their own poor? And what about loans that the IMF would know are destined to buy arms?

Before entering finally into the mechanism by which IMF could meet deficit needs, we must meet the policy questions just raised. Rather than try to take each up separately, we shall confine our attention mainly to austerity and, as occasion arises, comment on the rights, needs, and arms questions.

IMF and Austerity

IMF (as well as private lenders) require of their debtors the undergoing of correction or adjustment through cuts in imports, reduction of welfare programs, some unemployment. The question is how harsh is this in practice? Can it end in inducing the borrowing government to inflict repression when the ensuing austerity is resisted? Remember what the IMF goal is. It wants to prevent the country in deficit (on trade, tourism, debt service) from correcting this by the road of exchange controls or of protection.[23]

The loan accorded to avoid this route is presumed destined for productive activities which will fairly quickly restore the economy, with growth of production, income, employment and return to foregone services. It is, in short, a short-run affair.

How does the reduction of money supply and diminished fiscal activity bring on austerity? Less money means curtailment of credit, required in part to reduce importing. Some of this importing, of course, is carried on by businesses which may need imported materials for manufacturing. Governments will have to weigh whether this loss of production and consequent unemployment is required so that resources can flow more into more highly productive enterprises or into exports required to correct the trade deficit.

Fiscal discipline means cutting out welfare benefits. All this spells austerity. We have, then, two questions. First, is the austerity too harsh? And second, does the ensuing deflation really restore the debtor's economy? Which is to ask whether deflation may not breed further inflation?[24]

The case thus rests; if IMF conditionality is necessary, that is, if it is both efficacious and necessary, and provided the degree of austerity were more than compensated for by subsequent expansion of jobs and services for the poor, then it can be supported.

But two caveats appear within this hypothesis. First, the American people have made their own adjustment to increased costs of oil, not by any austerity, not even cutting back much on use of oil. They have made it by expanding international monetary reserves, which reflects their unwillingness to take the medicine they exhort others to gulp down. Instead of discipline, inflation; their choice of inflation against austerity ought to make them more sympathetic to the developing countries.

Their second caveat gives further reason for less harsh treatment. This is, as said earlier, that the developing nations are not responsible for the recession, inflation, floating exchange rates and oil hikes that have roosted at their doors.

But to return to IMF austerity, even within that as a given, it is still legitimate to press upon the Fund the promotion of human purpose—rights and needs of the poor. At the minimum the Fund must not give support to present inequities within the national security states of the Third World.

Admittedly this imposes certain political considerations on the Fund's operators. They might object that if the US imposes its rights/needs program, then other members may impose measures unpalatable to the US. But it seems legitimate to require certain minimum human considerations even while acknowledging that political realities may not permit them to be as operable as one desires. Admittedly, others might use the rights/needs program to justify other political considerations of their own.

There are other minimum considerations. The Fund should see to it that austerity is not, so far as they can see to it, borne only by the poor; also that small local businesses are not fundamentally hurt by a policy of supporting export business. It must be sensitive to the fact that its required deflation hits hardest the poor and maybe not at all the rich exporting sector.

Our second question on austerity is whether it works. It is alleged by some that the program which entails austerity is so deflationary that it causes, not expansion, but continued deflation with its accompanying unemployment. Deflation (the opposite of inflation) is achieved by reducing credit and fiscal spending. We have seen the reasons for requiring this. But we should add that it is needed in order to offset inflationary tendencies which may accompany devaluation of local currency. This devaluation is proposed in order to make it more attractive for foreigners to buy the devaluating country's exports. All that is good, but it may be that deflation creates a psychological environment for local business of doubts about the recuperability of the country. True both IMF as well as private bank experience seems not to warrant this allegation. Still one authority argues that "conventional austerity rarely facilitates effective long-term response." Others point out that many of these countries have already undergone significant reduction in their standard of living. To how much more must they be submitted?

A New Role for the IMF

Here we face the question of whether IMF terms are excessively harsh, and if so whether mechanisms cannot be created to soften them. To begin with, for several reasons, other sources of financing than banking or other private capital must be found. Demand for loans will rise at the very moment that private banks are stabilizing their loans. The World Bank estimates that a 6% annual average increase will require a 5% annual increase of lending. Moreover, that need will come in the early 1980s at a time in which past loans will massively present themselves for payment. Thus there will be a higher debt service ratio to growth in GNP than presently, motive for seeking further and larger loans. (The industrial countries, needless to say, would not be happy if that financing were not forthcoming, for lack of it would dry up Third World buying of the North's products.)

So a shift is in the making toward more public lending, bilateral and multilateral with focus on the latter. Nor is this latter a mere matter of a Witteveen facility of $10 billion, for that meets only a part of the vast need. It will require that the IMF become at the world level the equivalent of the national authority which accepts debt to prevent domestic unemployment.

Apart from amounts of money, at the heart of the program must be terms of credit consistent with the peculiar nature of the South's debt. We need not repeat our description of it. Much of the short-term loans (which in the 1974–1980 period really should have been longer term) will be replaced by longer term and additional financing. While the middle-income countries will be expected to accept sacrifices, they will not be subjected to shortages in financing. And why?

Our analysis of the debt situation reveals that it is beyond any normality. True, as we pointed out earlier, important borrowers have paid on time. Some even earlier than required. But all indications are that this will not easily be the case come 1985, as service payments grow. Equally, we may not forget the sacrifice undergone—cut in imports essential to development, and probably—disturbing to us—reduced imports from the United States.

If the debt situation is indeed beyond any normality something different from normal tests of credit worthiness should govern. (One does not expect private banks to be able to meet these. Hence while retaining their significant role in the debt partnership, they will hold a lesser role than today.) Longer term credit will be the order of the day, for, in our judgment, economic adjustments need not and should not be demanded over such short ranges of time as presently. Moreover, for those who seek a better deal for the poor of the Third World, it seems certain that short-term adjustment, at least in present circumstances, precludes realization of that goal. [25]

What the IMF must do, many experts believe, is two things: Shift some of the risk of debt from debtors to creditors through IMF financing, help create new financial instruments which permits longer term payment of debt.

This brings us to the newest creation of the Fund. Experts

agree that the $10 billion facility will help, especially those countries that cannot meet conditionality of the private banks. Apart from this complementarity it provides another service— establishing credit worthiness so that IMF borrowers can approach private sources. But it has its limitations. It is a one-shot injection. It is resolutely on a country-by-country basis. But apart from not remotely meeting the financial needs of the debtor nations, its main defect is that it does not raise its sights. It gives no assurance of longer-term lending, easing of conditionality, recognition of the service-carrying problem of non-oil producing debt.

New Approaches to Debt

Some of these turn on IMF and/or the World Bank. Some on OPEC. Some combine OPEC with OECD. And other combinations are possible.

1. *How To Increase Credit Capacity of the IMF?* A first suggestion is that, like the World Bank, the Fund be permitted to go out into the market, exchanging its bonds for investment funds. The funds collected could then, as in the case of the WB, be lent to those countries which could on longer term lending effect gains in development. However, the corresponding type of WB loans are at rates of interest close to those of the private market. If IMF followed that pattern, it would not respond to the need.

A second suggestion is the enlargement of IMF quotas. This proposal supposes that allocation of the enlargement would favor the Third World's non-oil producers. This proposal recalls the link proposed in UNCTAD III, 1972, between SDRs and Third World development. The SDRs would be cycled through the hands of the needy who would spend them on imports, thus placing them into the required pool of trade finance. This is analogous to the Marshall Plan and merits serious attention. For the situation of the non-oil states is not dissimilar to that of a prostrate postwar Europe. (All these proposals are of course in addition to the March 11 UNCTAD proposals for virtual or entire debt conversion to grants for the least developed and of serious study as to what to do for the middle-income states.)

A still more imaginative proposal for enlarging IMF capacity is that the IMF take over that part of private debt which banks and other private sources may for reasons discussed above no longer desire to carry. Since this would presumably be an accommodation for the banks they would be prepared to accept a lower rate of interest than they are presently charging for the loans they would give up. The IMF could then renegotiate with the developing countries, offering lower rates and longer terms, thus transferring short term into long term debt.

2. *OPEC Responsibilities.* Still other proposals are based on the analysis, already seen, which lays at the door of OPEC a large part of responsibility for the debt plight. Some call for a two-tier price system; lower prices for the poor nations; higher prices for the rich industrial world, which would thus bear the burden of meeting oil depletion requirements. A second is that OPEC take over directly solution of the problem it created. It would transfer financing directly through loans and grants, and not by depositing its surplus in banks. This could be done via IMF.

Several combine two or more of the above. One stems from the noted Balliol economist, Lord Thomas Balogh. In *Development Forum*, January–February 1978, he proposes in addition to grants from OECD to the poorest:

a. A graduated preferential scale (equivalent to the two-tier pricing).

b. The linking of SDRs with international aid by giving them preferentially to the least developed instead of issuing them in accordance with existing national quotas.

c. A lesser role for private financing.

3. *OECD/OPEC Roles.* As with Balogh's proposals, several other experts combine the roles assigned above to OPEC together with an OECD role of larger component of grant in its giving and more sustenance of IMF funding for debt financing. In addition, these exhort the OECD group not to throw off the problem of their oil deficits onto the developing nations. This they do, as we have seen, by refusing to attack their oil deficits by the discipline of reduced petroleum imports. Presently the North prefers to rely on the Third World to maintain its indebtedness at whatever cost so long as it enables them to continue buying the exports of the industrial world.

4. *And Then the Radicals.* Let the world financial system collapse. There is no other way of making OPEC confront its responsibilities or the industrial world to recognize that it could by retrenchment do something about its deficits instead of plunging the world into a sea of paper money. Some go so far as to invite developing country debtors to repudiate their debts in the belief that this could start the inevitable and necessary collapse.

CONCLUSION

We have seen several things:

1. Debt is more closely than ever linked to trade.

2. The foreign-held debt of the non-oil producing countries of the Third World is taking on astronomical dimensions.

3. The governments of the North Atlantic are gradually becoming aware of the enormity of the problem. Their official aid to the least developed will, hopefully, now take the form of grants.

4. The main problem is the vast quantity of debt held by the so-called middle-income countries. We have seen reasons why private holding of such debt will have to be diminished; this is partly because it is too short to meet the predicament of those countries. It is also because the sheer amounts ahead will require that the world community address itself to the problem.

5. In doing so, that community must recognize three things about the present debt situation:

a. Largely, it is not of the Third World non-oil producers' making.

b. OPEC bears large responsibility.

c. So does the industrial world. For two reasons. First, nearly half the debt problem involves food, fertilizers, industrial goods. Second, Third World debt keeps up spending for the North's goods, thereby removing the need, to a significant extent, of the North making its own austerity adjustment to oil prices.

6. A number of proposals thrust the IMF into the limelight. These we need not repeat here—but virtually all start with the proposition that the IMF must reduce the austerity it requires, and, second, that it will have to create more long-term lending.

7. In short, what is asked is that the IMF become what it is not—that International Monetary Authority that our times demand.

NOTES

1. Developing countries is a term requiring distinctions. At the first session of the UN Conference on Trade and Development (UNCTAD) in 1966 the developing nations adopted a term designated by their then number, the Group of 77. Now over 100, they still use that identification. They are also referred to as the Third World. Within this group distinctions must be made. The oil-producers, OPEC, while still developing nations are as a group rich. Still another group has emerged in Gross National Product from the stark poverty of underdevelopment. These are mainly manufacturers of export, as Brazil, Mexico, Singapore, Korea, and Taiwan. In this article I shall where suitable refer to the bloc of developing countries as the South, the Group of 77, the Third World. To designate the industrial nations of the North Atlantic plus Japan and Australia and New Zealand I shall frequently use North.

2. It has been suggested that OPEC earnings could be recycled in the same way or some combination of OPEC and industrial wealth.

3. Address to the Board of Governors by Robert McNamara, President of the World Bank, September 1977, p. 18.

4. Refer to *Annual Report for 1977*, p. 15.

5. McNamara adds that if the developing nations were to remove all constraints on export of their own manufactures they could by 1985 earn yet another $21 billion.

6. UNCTAD estimates the cost of the fund as around $6 billion for the ten basic commodities—cotton, rubber, hard fibers like jute and sisal, copper, tin, the tropical beverages of cocoa, coffee and tea and, finally, sugar. Three of these billions would be back-up for which funding could be deferred. The other three would come in the form of one billion dollars in paid up capital and the remainder in loans carrying interest charges.

7. *Hearings before the Subcommittee on Economic Stabilization of the Committee on Banking, Finance and Urban Affairs, House of Representatives*, June 8, 1977, p. 48.

8. *Ibid.*, p. 13.

9. Of course, an increase in the price of coffee may mean no gain for the people who make up the bottom 40% of the Colombian society. It may and does get stuck at the level of middlemen and owners. This untoward result might be avoided by pressuring governments of the Third World to a fairer distribution of the benefits of trade improvement even while con-

senting to agree to them. It should parenthetically be noted that price improvements would not help the poor world exclusively, since one-half of all commodities are exported by rich nations like the USA, Canada and Australia. For this reason UNCTAD focuses on the commodity trade that lies mainly in the hands of the developing nations.

10. From the side of the poor nations there is the same consideration against all other cartels as against OPEC. Those poor nations requiring the commodities under negotiation may be severely hurt by price hikes. One can think in particular of resource-poor South Asia with over a billion population.

11. *Hearings on Economic Stabilization*, p. 48.

12. *Ibid.*, p. 9.

13. *Ibid.*, p. 41.

14. *Ibid.*, p. 20.

15. *Ibid.*, pp. 48 and 49.

16. *Ibid.*, p. 50. Katz is not of course supporting the Third World's proposal on financing the CF through direct capital subscriptions by governments. He would finance the CF by pooling the cash resources of the separate buffer stock financings or by borrowing against callable capital or by borrowing against guarantees pledged to the CF by the individual commodity agreements. These latter would retain responsibility for their own financing. Testimony before the Subcommittee on International Economic Policy and Trade of the House Committee on International Relations, February 21, 1978.

17. A different way of totalling gives for the period 1974–1976 a total debt of $277. Of this private banks financed 46%, other private sources 34% and public sources 20%.

18. UNCTAD's Secretariat argues that the only reliable deflator of debt burden is one that reflects *terms of trade*; therefore that includes not just an export price index but also an import price index (TD/AC.2/4).

19. Seventeen of the 19 poorest countries are recipients of U.S. aid. These include Bangladesh ($153 million), Ethiopia ($109); Egypt ($700) is not listed among the poorest.

20. Some add another question: Will they be able to? One could imagine OPEC countries shifting their short-term funds out of US banks. One could imagine defaults that would cripple some banks thereby reducing enthusiasm for making money by lending so much to the Third World. Would defaults lead to collapse of the system? Some believe so. Most recognize that the Federal Reserve would shore up the system even though the FED might (and rightly) let some banks go down.

21. It does not seem appropriate that profit-making institutions should receive from their governments cost-free benefits. This seems the case at least for such US government operations as the Export-Import Bank which guarantees bank loans for export credits. Such guarantees ought to bear a premium. Some believe that in practice all bank loans to the Third World are guaranteed by the U.S. government. That is to say, that

while bankers profess to want to go it on their own, they know that in fact the US government faced by Third World default, at least if it be question of several, will lend to the potential defaulters, thus permitting them to pay the banks. Banks are multinational corporations, and like their producing and marketing counterparts are subject to criticism. Should banks lend to build more supertankers? Should they lend to produce goods of little or no value for the Third World?

22. The same questions have their relevance for banking and all other private business activity.

23. Some would say that this policy itself reflects the Fund's ideology which favors the maximum degree of free markets (exchange controls would be direct interference with markets) and of private enterprise (the deficit government will get a loan only if it agrees to support private initiative).

24. A further question is that raised recently by the Finance Minister of Portugal. He believed that IMF terms discussed in early 1978 were excessively harsh but finally accepted a $50 million IMF loan which will free up $750 million from other countries. His question was: given that the loan is a stop gap, and will have to be renewed, what assurance does Portugal have of such renewal?

25. For instance, while profits are lightly impacted, the adjustment tends to fall heavily on government expenditures for health and welfare.

BIBLIOGRAPHY

Friedman, Irving, *The Merging Role of Private Banks in The Developing World* (Citicorp, New York, 1979).

U.S. Subcommittee on Foreign Policy of the Committee on Foreign Relations of the United States Senate, *Staff Report on International Debt, The Banks, and US Foreign Policy* (U.S. Government Printing Office, Washington, D.C., 1977).

Wachtel, Howard M., *The New Gnomes: Multinational Banks in the Third World* (Transnational Institute, Washington, D.C., 1977).

Hughes, Helen, *The External Debt of Developing Countries*, in *Finance & Development* (December 1977, Washington, D.C.).

Polak, H. Joost, *Equitable Growth and the World Order* in *Finance & Development* (December 1977, Washington, D.C.).

Albert Fishlow, Richard S. Weinert, Marina V. M. Whitman,

Kenneth Lipper, Helen B. Junz, *The Third World: Public Debt, Private Profit*, in *Foreign Policy* (Spring 1978, Washington, D.C.).

McNamara, Robert, *Address to the Board of Governors* (Washington, D.C., 1977).

Discussion Questions

1. What is the model of development implicit in a strategy of reliance on multinational corporations?

2. What does Barnet mean by "progressive" development and what is the role of the multinationals in that model? What behavioral and structural changes would allow the multinationals to play a more vital role?

3. In what ways can we exercise our institutional imagination so as to create new organizations that combine serving the priorities of development and meeting basic needs with the attention to efficiency and innovation characteristic of transnational corporations?

4. Is there scope for existing transnational corporations to adapt to the needs of poor people, or is there an irreconcilable conflict? If adaptation is possible, what conditions would have to be met for successful adaptation to take place?

5. Can you think of any real basic needs goods, produced and marketed by transnational corporations, which are bought by the masses of poor people? If so, do you regard this as evidence against the thesis of this paper?

6. Is freedom of entry to industrial markets more important for the developing nations than price stabilization and/or price increase?

7. Is the debt of the non-oil producing Third World countries in any

significant way different now from what it was before the increases in price that began in 1972/1973?

8. Is IMF conditionality (austerity program) too severe?

9. Discuss one or other proposal for remedying the debt situation of the non-oil producing countries of the Third World.

VI
Further Theological Perspective

Theological Reflections
on Economic Realities

John Howard Yoder

For many of us the dominant impact of this encounter has been the force of the scientific model represented by the economists. Not all our authors have been economists by trade, but economics has been the language of our meeting. Economics conceived as a science operates with the assumption that the regularities it observes are not merely observable like those of astronomy but capable of manipulation like those of chemistry.

The question that had come to my attention on reading the preparatory materials surfaced again frequently in the course of the meetings. It lies at the intersection of two observations which arise when we bring the model of scientific manipulation into social experience.

The use of science in manipulating the processes of real history becomes a part of the larger power paradigm which as I already noted is part of the dignity but also the tragedy of humankind in general but especially of modern Western self-understandings. Taking control of history is perceived by most of us as self-evidently both a right and a duty. Historians of religion have recently been abundantly documenting the claim that this vision of history not merely as fate but also as task is a result of biblical faith, which tells us that a creator God had made reality meaningful and a provident God has made our efforts significant. Whatever be the contribution of biblical faith as over against cyclical or timeless religions of other cultures, certainly the notion that we both can and should control our history has been enormously fostered by other experiences as well; by the alliance of Christianity with civil control of society since Constantine and by

211

the enormous expansion of the physical potential for manipulating the world with the industrial and scientific revolutions of recent centuries. So we have been trained to assume that we both can and should run the world for good. In order to succeed in running the world we are willing to make some shortcuts and adjust our ethics, thus introducing the entire set of problems related to violence, manipulation, deception, and the calculus of ends and means. If we do not succeed in running history for good, we are angry at ourselves or/and others, with destructive psychic and social results.

Until now, economics being a science, we have assumed that the economists with a little more time would tell us how to make things work right. Yet the picture the economists give us now is one of very limited capacity to make things come out right, partly because the tools of economic analysis are not as scientific in the sense of generalizability and control as those of the chemists, and partly because of the many centers of power in the economic system which are not committed to the ethical concerns we are talking about.

The continuing ability to reason in terms of the power model is further undercut each time more complete and careful analysis shows us a point at which our discussion of desirable change is unrealistic. Numerous of these points come to the surface in our documents.

Albert Waterston reminded us that the very notion that a solution can or must be global is itself dysfunctional. It increases the overhead of the operation. Time and cost are invested in levels of planning which are wasted, the opportunity for confusion and corruption is increased, the tendency to ideology is a further source of tension, and instead of doing a job one concentrates on a debate about the reasoning behind doing it that way.

A more broadly visible pitfall in the papers is the way in which at crucial points the initiative is taken away or the buck is passed from the level of the economic system itself to other authorities or criteria which are not a part of the discussion. Beyond a certain point it does little good to decide what would be a better economic system if we know that the people in control of the present system have so much selfish interest in not letting it change and so much power that they can keep it from changing or at least defend it against head-on attack. The most obvious point where these papers run us up against that barrier implicitly or explicitly is that they cannot discuss how "we" (whether that means the United States or Bread for the World or the World Bank) can impose a more just economic system on parts of the world where the present rulers are not interested in more justice. We go on talking as if the improvements we are envisioning were accessible, without itemizing the countries to which they will in any case not apply.

A second characteristic of the modern models of analysis is that the mechanical or statistical models of the natural sciences assume a closed causal system. We know what constitutes a causal input and we do not expect the system to be moved by any other kinds of causes. But what if the resources available to the total system will never be enough to meet the needs that we have defined as imperative? Then the quantitative limits of the system pose a problem which the scientific model itself makes insoluble. Now what if we are clear that something could and in a moral sense must be done, but we recognize that political economies are administered by politicians rather than economists, so that the good insights we do have have little chance of being listened to? Then the system is closed in a qualitative way.

If we did not have a religious world view focused on progress and power, then the fact that the situation is empirically desperate might not be culturally a surprise or religiously a problem. Or to describe the intersection from the other side: Until we discovered the limits of material resources on a finite planet and until we became more aware that political control is in the hands of many who do not plan to use that power for the welfare of the most hungry, we were not shaken in our power progress thinking. It is thus only when the empirical pessimism of science's closed system and the theological optimism of our Western cultural imperative collide that we have a most specific problem calling for theological or spiritual resources.

How do you keep your courage up in a situation where the empirical disciplines attempting to analyze the situation give you no grounds for the optimism which for a millennium has been fueling your ethical concern?

There would be religious answers to that question. There are

Jewish and Christian understandings of providence which are far better able to deal with defeat and paradox than is the modern model with its rootage in Constantine and 19th century visions of progress. But in these sessions we did not focus our questions at that point, nor work toward those answers. We did encounter another element of response to the question, a model which was present in our spirits in more than one way. It might be called the Hubert Humphrey model, if we were to take our symbolic cues from the first evening. The model was represented in our circles not only by the memory of Senator Humphrey himself but also by the personal styles of commitment of Theodore Hesburgh and Albert Waterston. All three of these men possess the kind of personality which keeps on working as if commitment were meaningful and devotions were not wasteful, even in a context where the probabilities of payoff are very modest and the lead times for any particular victory are so long that a chance of success comes after, not before, the decision to stick with it. But we did not analyze what it is that could—or whether anything can—make these men (all well over 50 and accustomed to a degree of social recognition) models for a total culture needing to live for longer than they will with the discrepancy between the imperative of progress and the depletion of resources.

This was the question I found arising as I read the materials before the meeting and we can see that it has been with us throughout. I now add in addition my own arbitrary selection from the accumulation of further topics which the meeting itself disengaged.

One set of concerns focused around the thesis that although economics acts like a mechanically modeled science, it should not. This can be said very simply on theological grounds, namely that it degrades persons to think of them only as consumers or producers who will respond to the stimuli of price. This first level reaction is however by nature difficult to keep alive within the conversation, as it seems to the persons at home in the economic model to be a denial of something self-evident.

A more modest critique would be to claim that *some* specific axioms which have been taken for granted in the analysis of the economic system need not be self-evident. One example which came to the surface was the suggestion that in particular circumstances it may not be at all unthinkable that debts might be forgiven. The suggestion arose from economists talking about some of the unwise investments which had been made by banking institutions in economically unsound development perspectives, where the health of the total system might be fostered more by an explainable default than by continuing to accumulate on the record obligations which can never be met.

The biblical equivalent of such an institutional pardon in the sabbath year and Jubilee liberation and in the Lord's Prayer is evident: This was however not its source in our discussion. Would an economic theory allowing for forgiveness of debts at certain points really be any less scientific than one in which that option is excluded?

Another category of unresolved issues which we encountered has to do with the structure of reasoning processes within religious ethics for which the economic agenda was simply the immediate occasion. I can best illustrate with a specimen from the sub-group in which I participated. We observed that we are so much the product of our own culture that we use economics as a model for ethics when we are trying to bring ethics into economics. The particular discussion in our group had to do with how radical should be our criticism of a system which, although it can claim to work better than some other systems, is still seriously unjust at other points. Our economists reasoned in terms of cost benefit analysis, that we must make do with the best available options, half a loaf being better than none, a bird in the hand being better than pie in the sky (the mix of the labels from our proverbial past is my contribution, not theirs). Better do what you can than attempt what you can't. Certainly the models of analysis of the meaning of ethical behavior which we have learned from the mechanically modeled sciences have increased our ability to be realistic and responsible. But does utilitarian cost benefit analysis exhaust the ways we can do ethics? Or would there be other patterns of analysis?

The strongest expression of dissatisfaction with the models in our group came (I think it not improper to recognize that the participants brought to it the strengths of their several vocations) first from a Jesuit, who represents the strong tradition that some elements of morality are not negotiable, because morality is insight borne by a disciplined community hearing the sound only of its own drummer. Second, the same objection came from a bishop, whose calling it is to cultivate an overview of the identity and interests of a host of people in the most varied situations, especially of those among them who have no advocate. These two critics who attacked the kind of thought that is satisfied to work within the options made available by the system may stand in here for a longer roster of alternative nonutilitarian models of ethical deliberation: personalistic styles of appeal, interdisciplinary exercises, the search for rules from outside the system to break the autonomy of the system and to stand in as advocates for absent parties and future parties. We had no Marxist among us. It would have been good if we had had one, because of the neglected element of the biblical moral witness which the Marxist critique represents. A Marxist would have argued that the "utilitarian" view of our economists, wanting to help as they can, is itself in a paradoxical way apolitical, because it does not reach beyond the system to critique the system's assumptions.

A third issue regarding the shape of ethical reasoning was dramatically represented by the image of the elevator on a sinking ship. The world economic system, we were told, with the North Atlantic industrialized economics as the engine room, is gradually losing headway and taking on bilge in ways which classical progress indicates only partially hide. Within that system we ourselves can see progress at certain points, but that is the deceptive progress of those who are in an up elevator on a sinking ship. Since, however, the up elevator can never go much farther up, is it the duty of the wise economist who knows the most about why the ship is sinking to stay with us in the elevator? Or should he be a revolutionary on the bridge taking control away from the incompetent captain? Or should he be a troubleshooter in the engine room getting the pumps to work better, leaving the room in the elevator for the women and children who are supposed to get on the lifeboats first? Or might the transition to life boats, i.e., to a fundamentally different economic system viable when the old one founders, be the first need?

Within the tools of analysis of the kind of economics we had been learning about during the weekend seminar, it is obvious that no other available system seems to be ready to replace the one we have. But the more we are told by our experts that the apparent adequacy of the present "free world free market economy" is deceptive, the less we can be content with the older assumptions that an unseen hand will make it work better than anything else after all in the long run, subject only to those manipulations which make the system do its thing better. At what point do the efficacy calculations of traditional analysis refute themselves, not because ethicists doubt them but because they don't work? Beginning with the inquiry after alternative styles of moral discourse we are driven to ask more than the present conversation found time for about alternative styles of economic vision.

Lastly, I note by way of record that at many points our discussions could well have sent us off to other agendas which would have called for a different kind of study process dealing with other matters than the economics of growth. Most especially the need became increasingly visible for Christians and other men and women of goodwill to see themselves not simply as parts of one macrosystem but also as members of an alternative or a minority community cultivating alternative value options, experimenting with alternative lifestyle visions, and socializing the kinds of persons whose infiltration of this system or that can make a difference.

If it should be the case that to go on working against the odds with very limited short-range positive reinforcement is deemed to be evidence of a desirable personality type, or represents the kind of attitude most likely actually to achieve something in the longer run, then it should be important to know what kinds of family life, what kinds of experiences in childhood and youth and what kinds of education facilitate the development of that kind of personality. Some of us may not consider this a "theological" question in the narrow sense but it certainly is an ecclesiastical one, and for us in Notre Dame it is a professional one: one that past assumptions about the adequacy of the total social system of Christendom to socialize the leaders of the next generation have not adequately resolved.

Thus a first need is for a believing community as the seed bed of persistent personality.

Second, if we are to take seriously the loss of privileged status and consensus in the culture at large, we shall need to give more attention than we have explicitly done in the past two generations to the function of committed communities as reference groups or strategy consultants and as support groups for those whose involvement in wider not very hopeful causes would otherwise become too lonely to bear. The resurgence of interest in ethnicity, as a value which Catholic culture had brought into our society until recently, is ambivalent in detail but is one concretion of the function here identified: A group smaller than the total society, committed to convictions as to morality and style to which not all can be forced to subscribe, is a prerequisite of significant minority leadership involvement. It is a shame that the models of that kind of minority identity which we have had in recent memory have been limited to groups whose specific commitment was to their own advancement in the social mix, rather than to an alternative vision of how the global community should be structured.

But the initial perplexity which the first draft reading of the papers provoked in me was not the division of labor between economists and religion but between economists and politicians. Repeatedly in our authors' description of what it would take to have valid growth, the sticking point was not a lack of notions about an approach which would be better than those thus far attempted but the fact that local political leaders to whom the United States or the World Bank or Bread for the World cannot give orders, will for their own reasons of both selfishness and ideology not permit those kinds of more healthy development. Our very readiness to meet here to discuss what would be a better pattern of development seems thus to be a carry-over from an earlier age when people could meet in the North Atlantic world and decide how the rest of the world should develop because they were effectively in charge whether directly as its colonial masters or indirectly as its neo-colonial market managers. As the development of new nationalisms, most of them following the direction of the national security state rather than growing democracy, decreases the space for both local and external moral critique, we face the fact of our powerlessness as we have not done before. How many problems have we not dealt with in the past by saying,

"There must be something we can do," itself a reflex from the epoch of mastery which some people call the Protestant ethic and others the social control paradigm.

Thereby I have begun to turn to the question of resources for explaining our priorities and motivating our involvement in causes where an assured payoff is not in sight.

For one set of people, it is the peculiar contribution of religious perspective to provide opium in such a situation. We need to stretch our cultural imagination just to be sure that the opium imagery is correctly understood. For Puritans, alcohol and opiates are wrong because they make people irrational or because they are consumed by the wrong kind of people, or because their use is pleasurable, or because it is deceptively pleasurable, or because they are habit forming. The shadow of moralistic condemnation under which "opiates" in this broader sense fall in Protestant-capitalist culture leads us to misunderstand what was meant by the initial adoption of this imagery in Marxism. The meaning being referred to is none of the above. The meaning that matters is focused at two other points, one of them actually positive in evaluation and the other negative for different reasons than those already indicated.

When a situation is genuinely hopeless, it is a genuine need of the human organism, whether individually or socially, to have some way to kill the pain. In a painful situation which cannot be remedied there is no virtue in enduring the pain if a pain killer is available. To be the victim of incurable pain is not a model from which to generalize, but when an individual is in that situation there is no moral ground for rejecting opiates. For a society as well the judgmental condemnation of opiates by people who are in better circumstances is to be challenged. It would be a good thing, not a bad thing, if in a concentration camp there could be pain killers.

The second characteristic of the opiate is the one which is negatively qualified by Marxists, and properly so: It is that opium decreases or destroys the ability to function to change one's situation. In this sense religion has sometimes functioned as opiate in the past, and Marxism is right for denouncing it at this point. But it needs also to be said that this is not the intended function of biblical religion, nor the function it actually discharged in major formative periods in the past. Therefore the possibility is not excluded that biblical religion might again work not as a soporific but rather as a stimulant.

Appendix

Status of Institutions Arising from the World Food Conference

Frederick C. McEldowney

In November 1974, slightly more than four years ago, representatives from 131 nations and more than 50 international organizations met in Rome at the World Food Conference. The conference was convened in an atmosphere of crisis, in the midst of a downturn in world agricultural output and widespread famine, particularly in the Sahelian zone of Africa and on the Indian subcontinent. As a result, the conference received a large amount of publicity, with a spate of reports both on the meeting itself and on the issues raised in the course of its deliberations.

Today the flow of reporting on world food problems has fallen off to a trickle. Without careful attention it would be easy to conclude either that the problem of hunger in the world has been eliminated by the fortuitous harvests of the recent past or that the problem has once again receded from worldwide attention to become a matter of worldwide neglect. Both pictures would be misleading. Instead, the impression gained from the vantage of daily contact with the course of international food policy is that while the world food situation is in most respects just as precarious as it ever was, the World Food Conference did help to set into motion a chain of events which affords the possibility of escape from international calamity, and perhaps even the hope of progress in combatting one of mankind's most ancient and persistent enemies, the scourge of hunger and malnutrition.

The most important result of the World Food Conference was the achievement of a broad consensus on the nature and scope of the world food problem and the general outlines of a strategy for solving it. This consensus is reflected in a series of 22 omnibus resolutions, in which the major conclusions are as follows:

1. The only way to solve world food problems in the long run is by increasing food production in the developing countries themselves, emphasizing those in which hunger is the greatest, but not neglecting those with the greatest potential for a rapid and significant increase.

2. Food aid, although essential in the short run, is basically a stopgap measure.

3. The resources devoted to increasing food production in the developing countries must be substantially increased.

4. An international system of grain reserves is needed.

5. Adoption of rational population policies is a vital part of the long-term solution.

Unfortunately, achievement of a consensus is an intangible result and passage of any number of resolutions on the subject of hunger will by itself do absolutely nothing to fill a single belly. Any number of attempts have been made to monitor progress in implementing the resolutions, but the time frame has been so short and the information available so limited that no firm conclusions are possible. For example, while resource flows for agriculture development, as measured by official development assistance, have more than doubled from $2.5 billion in 1973 to over $5 billion in 1976, this growth is considerably more modest when adjusted for inflation. No information on total flows, i.e., international investment, private direct investment, etc., exists (though it is safe to assume they are far short of requirements). While food aid has grown from 7.3 million tons of grain equivalent in 1973/74 to about 9 million tons in 1977, the amount is well below the 10 million ton minimum target set by the Conference, let alone peaks of the previous decade. Moreover, the recent increase may simply reflect a reversion to the cycle of growth in surplus and cutback in scarcity which has far too often characterized food aid programs. Similarly, though the convening of a negotiating conference for a new international wheat agreement in February 1977 gives cause for optimism that an international system of food reserves may be created, progress to this point has been very slow and whatever impact on the problem of hunger among the needy peoples of the earth is still both far in the future and uncertain.

Perhaps a better way to assess the impact of the World Food Conference is to examine the status of the international institutions created as a result of its recommendations. These are: the Consultative Group on Food Production and Investment in Developing Countries, the International Fund for Agricultural Development, and the World Food Council. Examining these institutions also affords some insight into how international organizations work as well as a means of tracing the evolution of certain food policy and development issues.

As the only body expected to directly contribute resources for agricultural development, the International Fund for Agricultural Development (or IFAD, as it has inevitably become tagged) was seen by many as the only tangible achievement of the World Food Conference. In addition to its providing funds exclusively for purposes of agricultural development, IFAD was viewed by Conference participants as distinctive in two respects. First, the Fund was to be created from contributions provided both by traditional aid donors and "all those developing countries that are in a position to contribute" (WFC Resolution XIII), i.e., those members of the Organization of Petroleum Exporting Countries whose income has increased substantially as a result of the rise in the price of oil and related products. Second, the fund was to be administered by "a Governing Board consisting of representatives of contributing developed countries, contributing developing countries, and potential recipient countries, taking into consideration the need for equitable distribution of representation amongst these three categories and ensuring regional balance amongst the potential recipient representations" (WFC Resolution XIII). The power-sharing provision was included in response to the feeling among developing nations that existing international financial institutions were dominated by the leading industrial nations.

In the course of a series of meetings held in May, June and September 1975, it was agreed that the initial pledging target would be the equivalent of one billion SDR's or approximately $1 billion, and that the fund would begin operations only after at least 75 percent of this amount was deposited in the form of instruments of ratification. At the Seventh Special Session of the United Nations in September 1977, Secretary Kissinger announced that Congressional authorization for a direct contribution to the Fund of $200 million would be sought, provided that other countries added their support for a combined goal of $1 billion.

In the course of four meetings from October 1975 to April 1976 it became apparent that a major stumbling block to the Fund's establishment was the relative shares to be contributed by the developed and the OPEC developing nations. The developed nations generally felt that there had been an understanding that each of these categories would make roughly equal contributions to the fund. The U.S. appropriations request contained the provision that there be "equitable burden-sharing among the different classes of contributers." In January 1976 the OPEC nations as a group announced a joint contribution of $400 million from the OPEC Special Fund. Through the same period developed country contributions reached and slightly exceeded $500 million. Thus a gap of roughly $100 million remained between the pledges and the target, with a number of contributions contingent on closing that gap.

At the same time that pledges were being received, a draft agreement for establishing the fund was drawn up. Among the major provisions of this agreement were an equal division of the 1800 votes of the Board of Directors of the Fund among so-called Category I (developed), Category II (developing contributors), and Category III (developing recipients) and the following statement concerning the priorities in use of the resources of the Fund:

1. The need to increase food production and to improve the nutritional level of the poorest populations in the poorest food deficit countries.

2. The potential for increasing food production in other developing countries. Emphasis shall be placed on improving the nutritional level of the poorest populations in these countries and the conditions of their lives.

Thus, to an extent unique among international organizations responsible for the disbursement of resources, the IFAD agreement contains the principle that poor countries in general, and the poorest members of the population in particular should receive priority consideration. The Draft Articles of Agreement were adopted by consensus in June 1976. Formal signature of the articles was delayed until sufficient pledges were received.

The pledging gap was narrowed and finally closed in the course of the summer and fall of 1976. This process was helped considerably by the announcement of a contribution of $20 million by Iran, as well as a decision by the UN General Assembly to allocate to IFAD $20 million from the UN Special Fund. On December 2, 1977, the U.S. announced that the conditions placed on its contribution had been fulfilled. Meanwhile, two other issues arose, namely the designation of a permanent site for IFAD and the election of its President.

While the process of depositing formal instruments of ratification continued, the issues of the Presidency and site as well as preliminary work on the organization and procedures of IFAD were discussed in a series of four preparatory meetings from September 1976 to June 1977. Agreement was reached rather quickly on the designation of Abdelmuhsin al-Sudeary of Saudi Arabia as President. Although both Iran and Italy extended offers to act as host governments for a permanent site for the organization, it was eventually agreed that the issue of a permanent location would be deferred until after IFAD had become better established and proven its long-term viability.

Aside from the drafting of Agreements with cooperating international institutions such as the FAO and existing financial institutions, and the organizational structure of IFAD itself, the most important organizational issue considered by the preparatory meetings was a report on the lending policies and criteria of the new organization. This issue produced sharp debate between richer and poorer developing countries on who should receive funds from IFAD. Although the subject may arise again, that report makes the following principal recommendations:

1. The fund will give special consideration to projects that increase the output of cereals and other basic foodstuffs within the producing country, those that deliver a major portion of benefits to small farmers and the landless, those that induce a larger flow of national resources to agriculture, and those that promote economic cooperation among developing countries.

2. The largest portion of the Fund's resources should be lent on highly concessional terms (1 percent, 50 year maturity, 10 years grace) with the remainder on either intermediate terms (4 percent, 20 years maturity, 5 years grace) or ordinary terms (8 percent, 15–18 years maturity, 3 years grace).

3. In view of its limited resources, the Fund would attempt to play a catalytic role in raising the proportion of national and international funding directed at improving the well-being and self-reliance of the rural poor.

On December 13, 1977, with the commencement of the first meeting of its Board of Governors, IFAD became operational. Initial project financing can be expected within the next few months. Thus the preparatory phase in the life of this institution has ended, but only after a considerable amount of effort and debate concerning the relationships between developed and developing countries and the proper role of an international lending institution in the context of balancing growth with equity. The much more difficult operational phase, in which the institution demonstrates its long-term viability and ability to make a unique and significant contribution to the process of international development, has of course just begun.

In contrast to the heavy capitalization and operational role of IFAD, the Consultative Group of Food Production and Investment in Developing Countries (CGFPI) was conceived with somewhat different objectives and *modus operandi*. The World Food Conference recommended that CGFPI be organized and staffed jointly by FAO, the International Bank for Reconstruction and Development (IBRD or World Bank) and the United Nations Development Program (UNDP). The main functions of CGFPI were seen as follows: "(a) to encourage a larger flow of external resources for food production, (b) to improve the co-ordination of activities of different multilateral and bilateral donors providing financial and technical assistance for food production and (c) to ensure more effective use of available resources" (WFC Resolution XXII). As subsequently established by the three sponsoring agencies listed above, the CGFPI consisted of a modest staff of 4–6 professionals housed in the World Band complex in Washington, D.C.

Since its creation the CGFPI has conducted four meetings, in

July 1975, February and September 1976, and September 1977. The meetings were conducted in an informal and substantially collegial style. Discussion focused on papers prepared by or under the auspices of the CGFPI Secretariat and was led by the organization's chairman, former U.S. Ambassador Edwin M. Martin. Among the topics discussed at these meetings were Secretariat estimates of resource flows for increasing agricultural production in developing countries, investment requirements for fertilizer and seed production, personnel shortages affecting project preparation and implementation, and a methodology for preparing national investment strategies for increasing food production.

While the analyses of resource flows in particular helped to close serious gaps in international knowledge, the most important work of the CGFPI has been the development and implementation of the concept of food investment strategies, or "food plans." These food plans differ from traditional agriculture sector planning, particularly project planning, and the agriculture portion of national development plans in two important respects. First, they seek to integrate needs, particularly nutritional needs, with resources, especially non-financial resources, while considering the merits of alternative production patterns, e.g., capital vs. labor-intensive techniques, irrigated vs. rainfed agriculture, and foodstuffs production vs. cash crops for export. Second, they seek to consider the impact of policy alternatives such as input and output pricing, including the relative prices of substitutes, and landholding patterns. CGFPI's fourth meeting in September 1977 discussed plans produced for Senegal and the Sudan and preliminary plans for Bangladesh and Honduras. Though varied in sophistication and completeness, in the opinion of many observers these plans were a significant addition to existing information which would be of substantial value in undertaking future investment decisions.

At CGFPI's fourth meeting, in accordance with an agreement made at the previous meeting, the three sponsors of the organization announced their intention to conduct an evaluation of the role of the CGFPI in order to determine whether the organization as presently constituted was able to fulfill its terms of reference. Of particular concern to both the sponsors and participants in the meeting was the question of how the preparation of food plans would be linked with the provision of resources necessary for their implementation. Some CGFPI participants, particularly those from developing countries, preferred a direct linkage between the preparation of food plans and their funding. In their view, the CGFPI was created to underscore the particular importance of agricultural development, and thus help them obtain more funds for agriculture both within their own governments and from international institutions and bilateral donors. They would prefer, for example, to use the CGFPI mechanism rather than the World Bank's consultative groups since members of planning and financial ministries tended to represent their countries to these groups and were likely to favor large infrastructure projects and neglect agriculture. They hoped that the effort and expense of preparing food plans would be justified by a relatively automatic funding of their proposals with as little modification as possible.

On the other hand, other participants, particularly those from developed countries, viewed such plans as an important element in the funding process. However, automatic funding of such plans was not feasible in view of the exigencies of budgeting and programming. Most donors, for example, have to submit project proposals far in advance of when funds are needed in order to receive authorizations from their legislative bodies. All have quite rigid criteria which must be met before funds for a particular project can be approved, and many of the projects in a plan might not meet such criteria. Moreover, most donors would be reluctant to give funds to a plan certain aspects of which they did not approve, and there was no vehicle for resolving differences between donors and the recipient.

The result of the sponsors' evaluation of the role of CGFPI is expected early in 1978. Until these recommendations are available, the future of the organization is very much in doubt. Whatever the outcome of the organization, it appears clear that many of the activities begun by CGFPI have sufficiently demonstrated their value that they would either be formally assumed by another body or informally incorporated into the thinking and procedures of all members of the international community concerned with the process of agricultural planning and investment.

In many respects the most ambitious role for any of the organizations recommended by the World Food Conference was envisaged for the World Food Council. The Council was charged with the following primary function (WFC Resolution XXII):

> The Council would review periodically major problems and policy issues affecting the world food situation, and the steps being proposed or taken to resolve them by Governments, by the United Nations system and its regional organizations, and should further recommend remedial action as appropriate. The scope of the Council's review should extend to all aspects of world food problems in order to adopt an integrated approach toward their solution.

The Council was formally established on December 17, 1974 by a resolution of the UN General Assembly. The primary focus of the Council's work is on annual meetings of a 36-member ministerial (i.e., cabinet-level) body based on geographical representation. The Council Secretariat was created with approximately 20 professional positions, led by an Executive Director. This position has been occupied since the inception of the Council by Dr. John A. Hannah, former Administrator of the US Agency for International Development. The first Council President, the formal head of the 36-member ministerial body, was Sayed A. Marei of Egypt; he was replaced at the conclusion of his term in June 1977 by Arturo R. Tanco, Jr., who is also the Minister of Agriculture in the Philippines. Headquarters for the Council are located in Rome, in office space in the FAO complex.

The first meeting of the Council, held in June 1975 in Rome, was in large part taken up with procedural issues, especially the matter of the rules of procedure for the organization. For the most part the official report of the meeting reflects a lack of consensus on the issues discussed, instead recording the views of "many delegates" (generally the developing country members of the Council) and "some delegates" (generally the minority views of the developed country members of the Council). In accordance with agreed procedure, this report was adopted and forwarded through the Economic and Social Council to the UN General Assembly.

In an effort to improve upon the results of the first session, a preparatory meeting was called for May 1976, approximately four weeks in advance of the ministerial session. The purpose of this meeting was to dispose of routine, non-controversial and procedural matters so that ministers would not have to be concerned with them. To some extent this effort was successful. Laboriously negotiated draft rules of procedure were agreed upon and recommended to the ministerial session and the substantive issues of requirements for agricultural development, food aid policy and actions to improve world food security framed for ministerial consideration in terms which were generally acceptable to the members of the Council. However, on the last day of the session a set of draft resolutions, consisting essentially of a catalogue of demands, was tabled by the developing country members of the Council. Thus the preparatory session concluded by forwarding to the ministerial session two unrelated documents: a draft set of recommendations prepared by the Council as a whole, on which a number of members recorded reservations; and a set of resolutions proposed by the developing country members but not debated for lack of time.

When the Second Session was convened at the ministerial level, the results of the preparatory meeting eventually became the results of the session itself. The meeting split into a plenary session, which discussed the issues raised in the recommendations of the preparatory meeting, and into a committee of the whole, which tried without success to reach a compromise on the developing country resolutions. In the end the Council endorsed the report of the preparatory meeting and referred the recommendations as agreed therein (i.e., with reservations) to the relevant bodies and agencies of the UN and the governments of member states. The resolutions by the developing countries were noted by the Council, appended to its report, and forwarded to the Economic and Social Council for consideration.

The result was sustained through the Economic and Social Council to the UN General Assembly. In the General Assembly, the report was accepted as presented, but with the provision that the resolutions of the developing countries be given "sympathetic consideration" by the organizations of the UN system.

For the third session, it was decided that the practice of convening a preparatory meeting in advance of the ministerial session would be continued. At the same time the Council Secretariat conducted consultations with members on the agenda and the issues contained therein. These steps were taken in hopes of improving prospects for a favorable outcome. The agenda included items on increasing food production in developing countries, world food security, food aid, nutrition and food trade. The Secretariat documents prepared for these topics contained a set of draft recommendations for consideration by the ministerial session.

The Preparatory Meeting for the Third Session was convened May 19–24, 1977, in Rome. The United States delegation attended the session with the hope of focusing the deliberations more clearly on the problem of hunger and malnutrition, i.e., the needs of the poorest members of society, rather than attempting to present ministers with general recommendations on the full range of international food problems. Meanwhile, after the first day's session the developing country members of the Council once again tabled its own set of draft resolutions, which were both less balanced and more extensive than the Secretariat draft recommendations. These two initiatives clearly worked at cross-purposes, and as a result the entire meeting was thrown into a turmoil from which it never really recovered. Further confusion was added by the great interest on the part of some relatively well-off developing countries in using the meeting as a platform for their complaints against the agricultural trade practices of certain developed countries, particularly the members of the European Community. The unsatisfactory result of this confusion was a set of 51 wide-ranging and vague recommendations containing a large number of reservations by particular members, rather than a concise narrowing of issues for ministerial consideration. Nevertheless, under the surface of the vague and confusing final product, which was generally recognized as unsuitable for ministerial attention, there was limited success in narrowing differences on some issues. In addition, the meeting reached a considerable level of agreement on the importance of nutritional need to increase the attention devoted to nutrition by international organizations dealing with food and agricultural problems. This topic had been neglected in previous international meetings since the World Food Conference.

The Third Session of the Council was convened in Manila June 20–24, 1977. The U.S. delegation was led by Agriculture Secretary Bob Bergland, the first time that an American cabinet member had attended a Council session. In the course of the meeting Secretary Bergland delivered a major address outlining recent U.S. initiatives in the field of food policy, including steps taken to improve the developmental effectiveness of U.S. food aid. A decision was made to contribute 125,000 tons of grain to a 500,000 ton UN emergency grain reserve, and measures to create a U.S. domestic grain reserve in advance of negotiation of an international system of reserves. The statement was widely commended and was regarded by many as having set a favorable tone for the Council session.

The most significant product of the Third Session was a document entitled "Manila Communique of the World Food Council: A Program of Action to Eradicate Hunger and Malnutrition." The Communique contains 22 wide-ranging but relatively clear and concise recommendations which address each of the major substantive topics on the agenda. In many cases compromise on the recommendations was facilitated by the adoption of language substantially similar to that contained in the final Communique of the Conference on International Economic Cooperation, which ended in Paris three weeks earlier. Among the most important recommendations of the Manila Communique are those urging all countries to increase the level of resources devoted to agricultural development, international organizations to assist food priority countries in determining the resource and input requirements as well as policy constraints to be overcome in achieving a minimum 4% per annum growth rate in agricultural production, the conclusion of a new International Grains Arrangement by June 1978, introduction of nutritional improvement as a major objective in national development plans, and achievement of the 10 million tons food aid target in 1977/1978.

While the negotiations which produced this Communique

were lengthy and often spirited, they rarely descended to the level of bloc politics and were almost never rancorous. The Communique was adopted by consensus in the final meeting of the session.

Most of the participants in the Third Session were of the view that they had participated in a constructive meeting. For the first time, the World Food Council was able to achieve a consensus. The recommendations of the Third Session were speedily endorsed by both the Economic and Social Council and the General Assembly of the United Nations. These positive achievements assure the near-term viability of the Council and give it the potential to make an increasingly significant contribution to international deliberations on world food problems. The next session of the Council is planned for June 1978, in Mexico City.

By way of conclusion, two additional observations are in order. First, the deliberations of international organizations, particularly at the policy level, are in no way a substitute either for decisions at the national level or the thousands of decisions which are necessary in the course of development planning or project implementation. Such organizations do have a useful role to play, however, as barometers of official opinion, promoters of dialogue on issues which transcend national boundaries or individual circumstances, and to some extent as motivating agents. Finally, in promoting the concept of growth with equity in international political discussions the expectation of success should be limited. For the most part, consideration of this issue is transformed into a question of the relationship between growth in developing countries and in developed countries, rather than the more pertinent question of raising the living standard of the poor *vis-à-vis* the rich wherever they might reside. Thus any attempt to press the issue directly in international discussions is likely to lead to conclusions which assume that growth is equivalent to equity, or to North/South dichotomies.

Biographical Notes

RICHARD J. BARNET is Senior Fellow of the Institute for Policy Studies, an independent center in Washington, D.C., devoted to research on public policy questions, which he helped to found in 1963. He served as co-director of the Institute until this year. During the Kennedy Administration, he was an official of the State Department and the Arms Control and Disarmament Agency and a consultant to the Department of Defense. A graduate of Harvard College and Harvard Law School, he served in the Army as a specialist in international law and has been a Fellow of the Harvard Russian Research Center and the Princeton Center for International Studies, and a visiting professor at Yale and the University of Mexico. He is Foreign Affairs Editor of *Working Papers for a New Society*.

DENIS GOULET, a pioneer in the ethics of development, holds Master's degrees in Philosophy (St. Paul's College, Washington, D.C., 1956), and in Social Planning (IRFED, Paris, 1960), and a Ph.D. in Political Science (University of São Paulo, Brazil, 1963). He has conducted extensive field work in Algeria, Lebanon, Spain, and Brazil, and shorter studies in several countries of Africa, Asia, and Latin America. His major books are *Ethics of Development*, *The Cruel Choice*, *A New Moral Order*, *The Myth of Aid* (with Michael Hudson), and *The Uncertain Promise: Value Conflicts in Technology Transfer*. Aside from holding Visiting Professorships at the University of Saskatchewan, Indiana University, the University of California, and IRFED (Institut de Recherche et de Formation en Vue du Développement, Paris), in 1969 he was a Visiting Fellow at the Center for the Study of Democratic Institutions. After spending four years (1970–74) as a Research Fellow at the Center for the Study of Development and Social Change (Cambridge, Massachusetts), he is presently a Senior Fellow at Overseas Development Council.

KENNETH P. JAMESON has lived for three years in Peru, first as a Peace Corps volunteer in Huancayo and then as a Fulbright lecturer in Arequipa and in Lima. He is presently Associate Professor of Economics at the University of Notre Dame where he teaches courses in Economic Development with a concentration on Latin America. Mr. Jameson received his Ph.D. in Economics from the University of Wisconsin-Madison in 1970. He has published in a variety of journals in the area of economic development. His most recent article, entitled "Growth and Equity: Can They Be Happy Together?" appeared in *International Development Review*.

MARY EVELYN JEGEN, S.N.D., Executive Director of Bread for the World Educational Fund, 1976-1978, received her Ph.D. in History from St. Louis University in 1967. From 1967 to 1971 she taught at the University of Dayton. The next three years she spent in teaching and research in Europe and India, returning to the United States to work in the field of education on issues of justice and peace. She is now National Coordinator of Pax Christi— U.S.A.

PHILIP LAND, S.J., of the Oregon Province, is well known among Jesuits. After his doctorate and graduate studies in economic development at St. Louis and Columbia Universities, he worked for many years at the Institute for Social Order in St. Louis. He was professor of economics and social studies at the Gregorian University in Rome before undertaking responsibilities as senior staff researcher for the Pontifical Commission on Justice and Peace at the Vatican. He also was a leading figure in SODEPAX, the joint Vatican-World Council of Churches' committee on society, development and peace (in Geneva). He has published widely on social justice and global development. Recently he returned to the U.S. to become staff associate at Center of Concern in Washington.

FREDERICK C. McELDOWNEY, born in 1945, is a native of Jackson, Michigan. He is married, with two children. He received a B.A. in Economics from Albion College, Albion, Michigan, and an M.A. in Economic Development from Georgetown University, Washington, D.C. He has held positions with the Department of Health, Education and Welfare, the Department of Labor, and the Agency for International Development. Since joining the Department of State he has served in Libya, South Africa, and the Sultanate of Oman. In his present position he has prepared for U.S. participation in international conferences dealing with food and agriculture, particularly the Conference on International Economic Cooperation, the World Food Council, and the Food and Agriculture Organization of the United Nations.

LYLE P. SCHERTZ, Ph.D. is Acting Deputy Administrator for Economics in USDA's Economics, Statistics, and Cooperative Service. He received his B.S. and M.S. degrees from the University of Illinois in Agricultural Economics and his Ph.D. from the University of Minnesota in the same field. He has conducted and managed economic research both in private industry, where he worked as an economist with the Pillsbury Company, and in government, where he has held several positions in USDA since joining that agency in 1962. He worked on the Kennedy Round of Trade Negotiations for the Foreign Agriculture Service and led research on international trade and monetary affairs in the Economic Research Service of USDA from 1965 to 1967. In the five years that followed, he was active in the international development work of USDA as Deputy Administrator of the International Agricultural Development Service. When that organization was merged with the Economic Research Service, his responsibilities were broadened to include natural resource and rural development economics. In his present position, he oversees an economic research program ranging over all aspects of the food and fiber sector, natural resource conservation development, environmental quality, and human and community resource development in rural America.

PAUL G. SCHERVISH is currently a doctoral candidate in sociology at the University of Wisconsin-Madison and associated with the university's Institute for Research on Poverty. He is writing his dissertation on how levels and types of unemployment differ according to the degree of worker bargaining power associated with an employment position and the type of firm in which the position is located. He was ordained a Jesuit priest in 1975. He has traveled and studied in Peru, worked as a congressional aide for Robert F. Drinan, organized among the poor in Toledo, and taught sociology at John Carroll University. He has published articles in various sociology and theology journals.

PAUL P. STREETEN is Special Advisor to the Policy Planning and Program Review Department of the World Bank. Until September 1978 he was Warden of Queen Elizabeth House, Director of the Institute of Commonwealth Studies and a Fellow of Balliol College, Oxford. He was Deputy Director General of Economic Planning in the Ministry of Overseas Development, a Fellow of the Institute of Development Studies, and Professor at the University of Sussex. Among his publications are *The Frontiers of Development Studies* and *Economic Integration.*

ALBERT WATERSTON is Professor Emeritus of Economics at American University, Washington, D.C. He has held several positions with the World Bank and has travelled extensively in Latin America, Africa, Europe, Asia and the Caribbean for that organization. Presently he is trying to improve results obtained from agricultural and rural development in poor countries through a U.S. AID-financed project run by a non-profit organization, Governmental Affairs Institute, in Washington, D.C., of which he is President.

JAMES H. WEAVER received his B.S. degree from the University of Arkansas in 1955, served in the United States Air Force from 1955 to 1958, received his Ph.D. in Economics from the University of Oklahoma in 1963, has been professor of Economics at American University since 1963, and has served two terms as Chairman of the Economics Department. He was on leave with USAID from 1975–1977. He has published three books: *Modern Political Economy: Radical vs. Orthodox Approaches*, *The University and Revolution*, and *The International Development Association as a New Approach to Foreign Aid*. He recently completed a study of the effectiveness of the World Bank in benefiting the poor for the House Committee on Appropriations.

CHARLES K. WILBER, Ph.D. is presently professor and chairman of the Department of Economics at the University of Notre Dame, and has taught at Multnomah College in Oregon, the Catholic University of Puerto Rico, Trinity College in Washington, D.C., and American University in Washington, D.C. He has worked for the Peace Corps and the Interamerican Development Bank and has lectured before the Agency for International Development and Foreign Service Institute. Since 1969 he has been an Adjunct Senior Staff Associate at the AFL-CIO Labor Studies Center. He is author of *The Soviet Model and Underdeveloped Countries* and is working on a book with Professor Kenneth Jameson on the present crises in the American economy.

JOHN HOWARD YODER is presently Professor in the Department of Theology at the University of Notre Dame. He holds degrees from Goshen College and the University of Basel. Mr. Yoder has taught at Goshen College Biblical Seminary, at Mennonite and Protestant seminaries in Buenos Aires and Montevideo, and has been a guest professor in ecclesiastical history, Protestant Theological Faculty, at the University of Strassbourg. He has published numerous articles in the fields of Reformation history, Church renewal, and Christian ethics. Of special note is his book. *The Politics of Jesus,* published by Eerdmans (Grand Rapids, 1972).

BREAD FOR THE WORLD EDUCATIONAL FUND

Bread for the World Educational fund is an educational service on hunger and related issues. It was founded by Bread for the World, an interdenominational movement of Christian citizens who advocate government policies that address the basic causes of hunger.

Bread for the World Educational Fund does not engage in lobbying. It designs and conducts programs in collaboration with colleges, seminaries, church groups, and others. It reaches a larger audience through publication of educational materials.

Bread for the World Educational Fund
207 E. 16th St.
New York, N.Y. 10003
(212) 260-7000